Ludwig van

Beethoven

1770-1827

THE GREAT COMPOSERS
THEIR LIVES AND TIMES

Ludwig van
Beethoven
1770-1827

MARSHALL CAVENDISH
NEW YORK · LONDON · SYDNEY

Staff Credits

Editors
David Buxton BA (Honours)
Sue Lyon BA (Honours)

Art Editors
Debbie Jecock BA (Honours)
Ray Leaning BA (Honours),
PGCE (Art & Design)

Deputy Editor
Barbara Segall BA

Sub-editors
Geraldine Jones
Judy Oliver BA (Honours)
Nigel Rodgers BA (Honours), MA
Penny Smith
Will Steeds BA (Honours), MA

Designers
Steve Chilcott BA (Honours)
Shirin Patel BA (Honours)
Chris Rathbone

Picture Researchers
Georgina Barker
Julia Calloway BA (Honours)
Vanessa Cawley

Production Controllers
Sue Fuller
Steve Roberts

Secretary
Lynn Smail

Publisher
Terry Waters Grad IOP

Editorial Director
Maggi McCormick

Production Executive
Robert Paulley BSc

Managing Editor
Alan Ross BA (Honours)

Consultants
Dr Antony Hopkins
Commander of the Order
of the British Empire,
Fellow of the
Royal College of Music

Nick Mapstone BA (Honours), MA

Keith Shadwick BA (Honours)

Reference Edition Published 1990

Published by Marshall Cavendish Corporation
147 West Merrick Road
Freeport, Long Island
N.Y. 11520

Typeset by Walkergate Press Ltd, Hull, England
Printed and bound in Singapore by
Times Offset Private Ltd.

© *Marshall Cavendish Limited MCMLXXXIV,*
MCMLXXXVII, MCMXC

Library of Congress Cataloging-in-Publication Data

The Great composers, their lives and times.

   Includes index.
   1. Composers—Biography.   2. Music appreciation.
I. Marshall Cavendish Corporation.
ML390.G82   1987   780'.92'2 [B]   86-31294
ISBN 0-86307-776-5

ISBN 0-86307-776-5 (set)
   0-86307-778-1 (vol)

Contents

Introduction

Ludwig van Beethoven is considered to be the greatest composer of all time by both academic authorities and the general musical public. Even those who do not find his music to their particular taste cannot ignore his contribution to the development of classical music. Beethoven broke through the constraints of 18th-century music to create works of unequalled power and emotion. All 19th-century composers were influenced by his towering example, and even composers working in the late 20th century cannot ignore his achievements.

This volume sets Beethoven's genius in the context of his life and times. The Composer's Life *begins with a general account of Beethoven's life, then analyzes some aspects of particular relevance: his patrons, his friends and lovers and his lasting musical influence. The* Listener's Guide *discusses some of Beethoven's greatest and best-known works, including the Fifth Symphony, the Emperor Concerto and the Moonlight Sonata.* In the Background *places Beethoven's life within its historical environment: the flowering of the arts that took place in German-speaking countries around the year 1800; the career of Napoleon Bonaparte – first admired, then reviled, by Beethoven; the Hapsburg family, which dominated central Europe during Beethoven's life-time; and the developments in 19th-century medicine that formed the science that we know today. Beethoven has left us an enduring legacy of great music. By analyzing and describing his life and times, this volume ensures that this inheritance can be fully appreciated, admired and, not least, enjoyed.*

Composer's life

Beethoven's music, with its celebration of the capacity of humanity to overcome suffering and its depiction of the sense of calm when the struggle is over, reflects his own victory over the misfortunes of life. Beethoven's life began ideally as he was born into a musical family: both his grandfather and father were members of the choir of the Elector of Cologne. However, his father was a drunkard, neglecting the family and forcing young Ludwig to take responsiblity for his two younger brothers. By the time he was 30, Beethoven was the toast of Vienna as a composer and virtuoso pianist, and continued success seemed assured. But the unthinkable happened: by 1802 he knew that he would eventually lose his hearing – the most valuable, and seemingly essential, of a musician's senses. For a time Beethoven was in despair and seems to have contemplated suicide, but he fought back, abandoning his career as a pianist to concentrate on composing. His victory over deafness can be measured by the magnificent Ninth ('Choral') Symphony, composed at the end of his life when he was completely deaf.

Ludwig van Beethoven
1770–1827

Beethoven's story is one of personal triumph over tragedy and supreme musical achievement. A complex and brilliant man, no composer before or since has exerted greater influence.

Beethoven was born in this house, at 515 Bonngasse, Bonn, on 17 December 1770. Not surprisingly, his place of birth has been a focus of interest: this pencil drawing was made in 1889 by R. Beissel, 58 years after the death of the composer.

A modern photograph of the same house now accorded the status of a shrine, in addition to its main function as a Beethoven museum. The only major structural changes made since Beethoven was born, have involved enlarging it on the garden side and altering the roof.

ZEFA

Ludwig van Beethoven is generally considered to be the greatest composer the world has ever known, even by people for whom he is not a personal 'favourite'. But why should he be held in such regard?

Consider these facts: no other composer's work has contained as large a proportion of established master-pieces; Beethoven took music out of the 18th century and gave it a radical new direction, and in doing so broke many rules which were considered sacrosanct – but always for good musical reasons. Moreover, despite all that has happened since his death, his music continues to influence composers today.

Early years

For someone who was destined to be lionized by the aristocracy of his time, Beethoven's start in life was inauspicious. He was born in Bonn on 17 December 1770, the son of an obscure tenor singer in the employ of the Elector of Cologne. His father was said to be a violent and intemperate man, who returned home late at night much the worse for drink and dragged young Ludwig from his bed in order to beat music lessons into the boy's sleepy head. There are also stories of his father forcing him to play the violin for the amusement of his drinking cronies. Despite these and other abuses – which might well have persuaded a lesser person to loathe the subject – the young Beethoven developed a sensitivity and vision for music.

When, despite his father's brutal teaching methods, Ludwig began to show signs of promise, other teachers were called in. By the age of seven he was advanced enough to appear in public. A year or so later the composer Christian Gottlob Neefe took over his musical training, and progress thereafter was rapid. Beethoven must have felt immense pride when his Nine Variations for piano in C minor was published, and was listed later in a prominent Leipzig catalogue as the work of 'Louis van Betthoven (sic), aged ten years'.

In 1787 Beethoven met Mozart. Beethoven was visiting Vienna, a noted musical centre, and must have felt a little out of his depth for he was clumsy and stocky; his manners were loutish, his black hair unruly and he habitually wore an expression of surliness on his swarthy face. By contrast the great Mozart was dapper and sophisticated. He received the boy doubtfully, but once Beethoven started playing the piano his talent was evident. 'Watch this lad,' Mozart reported. 'Some day he will force the world to talk about him'.

Preparing for greatness

With the death of his wife the last steadying influence on Beethoven's father was removed. The old singer unhesitatingly put the bottle before Ludwig, his two younger brothers and his one-year-old sister. The situation became so bad that by 1789 Beethoven was forced to show the mettle that was to stand him in good stead later in life. He went resolutely to his father's employer and demanded – and got – half his father's salary so that the family could be provided for; his father could drink away the rest. In 1792 the old man died. No great grief was felt: as his employer put it, 'That will deplete the revenue from liquor excise.'

For four years Ludwig supported his family. He also made some good friends, among them Stephan von Breuning, who became a friend for life, and Doctor Franz Wegeler, who wrote one of the first biographies of Beethoven. Count Ferdinand von Waldstein entered Beethoven's circle and received the dedication of a famous piano sonata in 1804.

In July 1792 the renowned composer Haydn passed through Bonn on his way to Vienna. He met Beethoven and was impressed, and perhaps disturbed, by his work. Clearly, he felt, this young man's talent needed to be controlled before it could be developed. Consequently Beethoven left Bonn for good early in November 1792 to study composition with Haydn in Vienna. However, if Haydn had hoped to 'control' Beethoven's talent he was fighting a losing battle. Beethoven's music strode towards the next century, heavily influenced by the strenuous political and social tensions that ravaged Europe in the wake of the French Revolution. Haydn, who had been a musical trendsetter himself in his youth, found that Beethoven was advancing implacably along the same radical path.

Those first weeks in Vienna were hard for Beethoven. Opportunities were not forthcoming; expectations were unfulfilled. In addition it must have irked him, fired as he was by the current spirit of equality, to have to live in a tiny garret in Prince Lichnowsky's mansion. Soon, however, the Prince gave him more spacious accommodation on the ground floor, and, mindful of the young man's impetuous behaviour, instructed the servants that Beethoven's bell was to be

Salmer

Mary Evans Picture Library

A highly idealized portrait of Beethoven (above), painted in 1819 by Joseph Carl Steiler, when the composer was 49 years old. He is shown at work on the score of the Missa Solemnis. *By this time he was already totally deaf.*
Beethoven was deeply attached to his mother, Maria Magdalena (left), referring to her as his 'best friend'. She died in 1787 of tuberculosis, when Beethoven was 17. A pious and conventional woman, she tried to shield Beethoven and her other children from their drunken father's worst excesses.

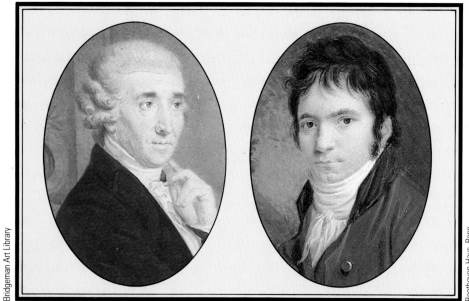

Bridgeman Art Library

Joseph Haydn (above), the great classical composer, attempted to guide the young Beethoven's talent; the latter, however, would have none of this and later claimed to have learnt little from his mentor. The miniature (above right) shows Beethoven in 1803, while he was composing the 'Eroica' Symphony.

for him to set up in his own apartments. He was the first composer to become a freelance by choice, as opposed to depending on patrons. However, it was his skill as a pianist rather than as a composer that brought him recognition during his twenties.

The onset of deafness

Beethoven's career as a virtuoso pianist was, however, soon to be terminated. In a letter written to his friend Karl Ameda on 1 July 1801, he admitted he was experiencing signs of deafness.

'How often I wish you were here, for your Beethoven is having a miserable life, at odds with nature and its Creator, abusing the latter for leaving his creatures vulnerable to the slightest accident . . . My greatest faculty, my hearing, is greatly deteriorated.'

Beethoven-Haus, Bonn

Apparently Beethoven had been aware of the problem for about three years, avoiding company lest his weakness be discovered, and retreating into himself. Friends ascribed his reserve to preoccupation and absentmindedness. In a letter to Wegeler, he wrote:

'How can I, a musician, say to people "I am deaf!" I shall, if I can, defy this fate, even though there will be times when I shall be the unhappiest of God's creatures . . . I live only in music . . . frequently working on three or four pieces simultaneously.'

Many men would have been driven to suicide. Beethoven may indeed have contemplated it. Yet his stubborn nature strengthened him and he came to terms with his deafness in a dynamic, constructive

answered even before the Prince's own!

Impetuosity was also a feature of his piano playing at this time. In those days pianists were pitted against each other in front of audiences to decide who could play the more brilliantly and improvise the more imaginatively. Beethoven's rivals always retired, bloodied, from such combat. While he made enemies of many pianists in Vienna, the nobility flocked to hear him. Personally and professionally his future looked bright. Compositions poured from him and he gave concerts in Vienna as well as Berlin, Prague and other important centres. His finances were secure enough

Therese, Countess von Brunswick (right), was Beethoven's pupil and developed an 'intimate and warm-hearted' friendship with him. She also gave him this portrait. This gesture has been suggested as evidence that she was his 'Immortal Beloved': the great and secret love of his often stormy life.

Salmer

way. In another letter to Wegeler, written five months after the despairing one quoted above, it becomes clear that Beethoven, as always, stubborn, unyielding and struggling against destiny, saw his deafness as a challenge to be fought and overcome:

Free me of only half this affliction and I shall be a complete, mature man. You must think of me as being as happy as it is possible to be on this earth – not unhappy. No! I cannot endure it. I will seize Fate by the throat. It will not wholly conquer me! Oh, how beautiful it is to live – and live a thousand times over!'

With the end of his career as a virtuoso pianist inevitable, he plunged into composing. It offered a much more precarious living than that of performer, especially when his compositions had already shown themselves to be in advance of popular taste. In 1802 his doctor sent him to Heiligenstadt, a village outside Vienna, in the hope that its rural peace would rest his hearing. The new surroundings reawakened in Beethoven a love of nature and the countryside, and hope and optimism returned. Chief amongst the sunny works of this period was the charming, exuberant Symphony No. 2. However, when it became obvious that there was no improvement in his hearing, despair returned. By the autumn the young man felt so low both physically and mentally that he feared he would not survive the winter. He therefore wrote his will and left instructions that it was to be opened only after his death. The 'Heiligenstadt Testament', as it is known, is a long, moving document that reveals more about his state of mind than does the music he was writing at the time. Only his last works can reflect in sound what he then put down in words.

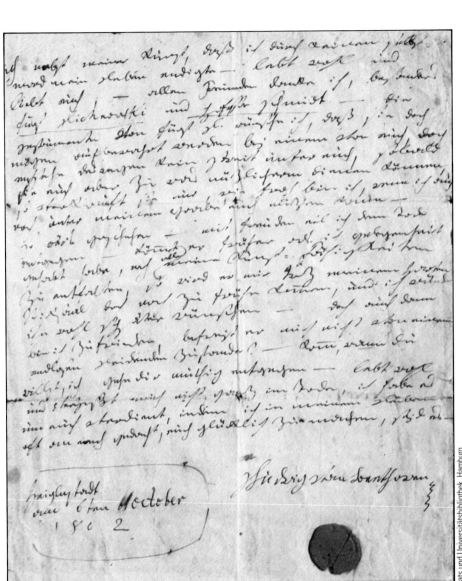

During the summer of 1802 Beethoven stayed in Heiligenstadt (left), a little village outside Vienna.

The last page of the 'Heiligenstadt Testament' (above), which Beethoven intended to be both a will and a statement of his personal philosophy. By now his deafness was developing and he felt he was soon to die.

'O ye men who accuse me of being malevolent, stubborn and misanthropical, how ye wrong me! Ye know not the secret cause. Ever since childhood my heart and mind were disposed towards feelings of gentleness and good will, and I was eager to accomplish great deeds; but consider this: for six years I have been hopelessly ill, aggravated and cheated by quacks in the hope of improvement but finally compelled to face a lasting malady . . . I was forced to isolate myself. I was misunderstood and rudely repulsed because I was as yet unable to say to people, "Speak louder, shout, for I am deaf" . . .

With joy I hasten to meet death. Despite my hard fate . . . I shall wish that it had come later; but I am content, for he shall free me of constant suffering. Come then, Death, and I shall face thee with courage. Heiglnstadt (sic), 6 October, 1802.'

Just how bad was Beethoven's plight? At first the malady was intermittent, or so faint that it worried him only occasionally. But by 1801 he reported that a whistle and buzz was constant. Low speech tones became an unintelligible hum, shouting became an intolerable din. Apparently the illness completely

One of Beethoven's most important patrons was the Russian Ambassador to Vienna, Count Razumovsky, to whom he dedicated a number of pieces. Beethoven is shown here playing for the Razumovsky family. On the right is their palace in Vienna.

swamped delicate sounds and distorted strong ones. He may have had short periods of remission, but for the last ten years of his life he was totally deaf.

Beethoven in maturity

The mature Beethoven was a short, well-built man. His dark hair went grey, then white, but was always thick and unruly. Reports differ as to the colour of his eyes. His skin was pock-marked, and his mouth, which had been a little petulant in youth, later became fixed in a grim, down-curving line, as if in a permanent expression of truculent determination. He seldom took care of his appearance, and, as he strode through the streets of Vienna with hair escaping from beneath his top hat, his hands clasped behind his back and his coat cross-buttoned, he was the picture of eccentricty. His moods changed constantly, keeping his acquaintances guessing. They could never be sure that a chance remark might be misconstrued or displease the master in some way, for his powerful will would admit of no alternative view once he had made a judgement.

By nature, Beethoven was impatient, impulsive, unreasonable and intolerant; deafness added suspicion and paranoia to these attributes. He would often misunderstand the meaning of a facial expression and accuse faithful friends of disloyalty or conspiracy. He would fly into a rage at the slightest provocation, and he would turn on friends, dismissing them curtly as being unworthy of his friendship. But, likely as not, he

A portrait of Beethoven painted by Ferdinand Schimon in 1818–1819, when the composer was at the height of his fame.

would write a letter the next day or so, telling them how noble and good they were and how he had misjudged them.

A tempestuous life

After his return from Heiligenstadt, Beethoven's music deepened. He began creating a new musical world. In the summer of 1803 he began work on his Third Symphony – the 'Eroica'. It was to be a paean of glory to Napoleon Bonaparte and, like its subject, it was revolutionary. It was half as long again as any previous symphony and its musical language was so uncompromising that it set up resistance in its first audiences. It broke the symphonic mould, yet established new, logical and cogent forms. This was a miracle Beethoven was to work many times.

Stephan von Breuning, with whom Beethoven shared rooms, reports a thunderous episode in connection with the 'Eroica' Symphony. In December, 1804, the news arrived that Napoleon, that toiler for the rights of the common people, had proclaimed himself Emperor. In a fury, Beethoven strode over to his copy of the Symphony, which bore a dedication to Napoleon, and crossed out the 'Bonaparte' name with such violence that the pen tore a hole in the paper. 'Is he, too, nothing more than human?' he raged. 'Now he will crush the rights of man. He will become a tyrant!'

For the next few years in Vienna, from 1804 to 1808, Beethoven lived in what might be described as a state of monotonous uproar. His relationships suffered elemental rifts, his music grew ever greater, and all the time he was in love with one woman or another, usually high-born, sometimes unattainable, always unattained. He never married.

His Fifth and Sixth Symphonies were completed by the summer of 1808. The Fifth indeed 'takes fate by the throat'; the Sixth ('Pastoral') is a portrait of the countryside around Heilingenstadt. These and other works spread his name and fame.

In July 1812 Beethoven wrote a letter to an unidentified lady whom he addressed as 'The Immortal Beloved'. It is as eloquent of love as his 'Heiligenstadt Testament' had been of despair:

'My angel, my all, my very self – a few words only today, and in pencil (thine). Why such profound sorrow when necessity speaks? Can our love endure but through sacrifice – but through not demanding all – canst thou alter it that thou art not wholly mine, I not wholly thine?'

So moving an outpouring may well have resulted, at last, in some permanent arrangement – if the lady in question had been free, and if the letter had been sent. It was discovered in a secret drawer in Beethoven's desk after his death.

His brother Casper Carl died in November 1815. The consequences brought about something that neither the tragedy of deafness nor Napoleon's guns could achieve: they almost stopped Beethoven composing. Beethoven was appointed guardian of his brother's nine-year-old son, Karl – a guardianship he shared with the boy's mother Johanna. Beethoven took the appointment most seriously and was certain that Johanna did not. He believed her to be immoral, and immediately began legal proceedings to get sole guardianship of his nephew. The lawsuit was painful and protracted and frequently abusive with Johanna asserting 'How can a deaf, madman bachelor guard the boy's welfare?' – Beethoven repeatedly fell ill because

Among the exhibits in the Beethoven Museum in Bonn is his piano (above). He was a celebrated virtuoso on the instrument until his increasing deafness forced him to abandon playing.

As he strode through the streets of Vienna, deep in thought and unkempt in appearance, Beethoven was the picture of eccentricity and a delight to caricature. Some sketches such as the one (right) by Lyser were able to capture that determination which so strongly characterized the composer.

of the strain. He did not finally secure custody of Karl until 1820, when the boy was 20.

The Ninth Symphony ('Choral') was completed in 1823, by which time Beethoven was completely deaf. There was a poignant scene at the first performance. Despite his deafness, Beethoven insisted on conducting, but unknown to him the real conductor sat out of his sight, beating time. As the last movement ended Beethoven, unaware even that the music had ceased, was also unaware of the tremendous burst of applause that greeted it. One of the singers took him by the arm and turned him around so that he might actually see the ovation.

The final days

In the autumn of 1826 Beethoven took Karl to Gneixendorf ('The name,' said Beethoven, 'sounds like the breaking of an axe') for a holiday. A servant there has left a graphic picture of Beethoven the possessed genius as he worked upon his last string quartet:

'At 5.30 a.m. he was at his table, beating time with hands and feet, humming and writing. After breakfast he hurried outside to wander in the fields, calling, waving his arms about, moving slowly, then very fast, then abruptly stopping to scribble something in his notebook.'

In early December Beethoven returned to Vienna with Karl and the journey brought the composer down with pneumonia. He recovered, only to be laid low again with cirrhosis of the liver, which in turn gave way to dropsy. His condition had deteriorated dramatically by the beginning of March and, sensing the

At 3 pm on March 29, 1827, Beethoven's funeral took place in Vienna. The Viennese turned out en masse: at least 20,000 people crowded into the square in front of the Schwarzpanierhaus – Beethoven's last residence. There were eight pallbearers, dozens of torchbearers and a choir who sang to the accompaniment of sombre trombones.

orst, his friends rallied round: faithful Stephan rought his family and Schubert paid his respects.

Beethoven's final moments, if a report by Schubert's iend Hüttenbrenner are to be believed, were ramatic in the extreme. At about 5.45 in the afteroon of 26 March, 1827, as a storm raged, Beethoven's oom was suddenly filled with light and shaken with under:

Beethoven's eyes opened and he lifted his right st for several seconds, a serious, threatening xpression on his face. When his hand fell back, e half-closed his eyes ... Not another word, not nother heartbeat.'

Schubert and Hummel were were among the 20,000 eople who mourned the composer at his funeral hree days later. He was buried in Währing Cemetery; 1888 his remains were removed to Zentral-friedhof Vienna – a great resting-place for musicians – where e lies side-by-side with Schubert.

fterword

eethoven revolutionized classical music, breaking nany rules which had been considered inviolate for enturies. He influenced every succeeding major comoser. It's possible that he did not personally share the ofty ideals later generations have attributed to his nusic: indeed, at the height of his powers he shows a rightening self-centredness, saying 'Strength is the norality of the man who stands out from the rest, and t is mine.' But his work – the most powerful and mportant body of music ever to be put together by ne composer – is eternal.

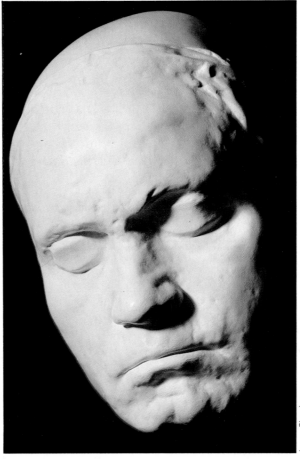

Two days after Beethoven's death the young painter Danhauser took this death mask of the composer. Parts of the temple bones had been removed at the post-mortem the previous day, giving the head a curious formlessness.

COMPOSER'S LIFE

Love and friendship

Beethoven never married, but not because he was uninterested in women. His lack of success in love can in part be explained by the realization that to him nothing mattered more than his art. Also his personality – impatient, impulsive and intolerant – would not have made an ideal husband, and certainly made him a difficult friend. His defects of character were not caused, but were magnified, by his loss of hearing. Unlike paralysis, deafness is an invisible disability and the deaf are sometimes thought stupid or withdrawn, causing them to react angrily – Beethoven himself complained of being 'misunderstood and rudely repulsed'. Despite the difficulties of his personality, Beethoven's friends were in the main loyal and their deep sense of loss on his death was summed up by the poet Grillparzer: 'It struck me like a sharp blow in my stomach, the tears sprang to my eyes.'

'My immortal beloved'

With his notoriously short temper and lack of domesticity, Beethoven hardly made an ideal friend or lover. This made his search for the perfect wife a succession of frustrated hopes.

Beethoven's nature was often observed to be both passionate and unpredictable. Indeed his old teacher Haydn once told him 'you give me the impression of a man with several heads, several hearts and several souls'. Behind this turbulence and perhaps the root cause of it, was an enormous reservoir of love, which was all-devouring and demanded total loyalty in return. With this went a sensitivity to any slight, whether real or imagined, and a tendency to be over-critical. Such overpowering emotions, which found their consummate expression in his music, could only be imperfectly realized in reality, perhaps most successfully with his friends. More emotionally demanding relationships with those of the opposite sex and members of his immediate family often proved disastrous. ·

His emotional make-up was exacerbated by his frustration and despair over his increasing deafness, the most disturbing aspect of his often chronic state of health. For a man already limited in his communications with others this could only have served to make him feel even more alienated from the everyday world. The anguish that he felt is made plain in the painful confession of the Heiligenstadt Testament found after his death (see page 11).

This emotional unsuitability for close relationships is echoed in his extraordinary lifestyle. Carl Czerny, one of Beethoven's most famous pupils described him as 'not being made for domesticity'. Many of his friends have attested to the extraordinary state of his rooms where one saw:

The chaos and disorder in which Beethoven lived were always a source of amazement to his visitors. Shown (above) in front of the house in which he stayed in Heiligenstadt, a village close to Vienna, it is obvious that his living conditions might not have suited a wife.

The deferential manner shown by the painter Waldmüller towards Beethoven (above) irritated the composer intensely, and resulted in this stern and glowering portrait.

. . . the greatest disorder and lack of cleanliness imaginable. On the old piano dirt and dust carried on a continual battle with written and printed sheets of music; underneath it was an unemptied chamberpot . . . chairs were covered with items of his clothing and plates containing the remnants of yesterday's evening meal.

This, combined with his distrust of servants with whom he was continually quarrelling or sacking, make it hardly surprising that he was often forced to change residence, sometimes several times a year. Such then was the personality and home environment ahead of a prospective wife.

Women

Indeed, Magdalena Willmann, a talented singer the composer had known from his Bonn days, brusquely rejected his proposal of marriage in 1795, roundly declaring later it was because he was 'so ugly – and half-mad'. Nevertheless Beethoven, perhaps mindful of Mozart's successful example, was to pursue the elusive phantom of the perfect relationship, the marriage made in heaven, for the next 20 years. His singular failure in realizing this is best summed up in his own words 'If I had spent my time on women and love, what would have come of my art'. It was as though this perfect ideal of love that he could express so well in his music, he never dared to put to the test in reality for fear that he might in doing so destroy the ideal. Perhaps this explains why he chose to woo women of aristocratic birth, whom he could never marry anyway because of his own low social standing, or women who were already married.

In 1799 Beethoven gave piano lessons for a brief period to the two young Countesses von Brunsvik, Therese and Josephine. Charmed by them, not only did he not miss a single lesson but often extended the lessons well beyond their limit. Thus began a close friendship with the family, Beethoven visiting them often at Korompa castle, their estate in Hungary. Through the von Brunsviks he gained another pupil, their cousin Giulietta Guicciardi with whom he became infatuated. This rather flirtatious young lady, to whom Beethoven dedicated his 'Moonlight Sonata' obviously enjoyed the power she had over her extraordinary teacher who was, moreover, twice her age. Instead of impressing her with his feelings, Beethoven's frequent vigils underneath her balcony window only served to amuse her. This infatuation ended when Giulietta married a composer, Count Wengel Robert Gallenberg, and left Vienna in 1803.

A more serious infatuation developed with Josephine von Brunsvik, who became widowed in early January 1804. She began taking piano lessons with Beethoven and he was a frequent visitor at her Vienna mansion, no doubt initially fulfilling and enjoying a paternal role in the Countess's family. From correspondence it seems evident Beethoven urged her for a physical consummation of their relationship, a request to which Josephine, despite her obvious fondness and concern for the composer, was not prepared to acquiesce. Nevertheless the friendship continued until 1807, proving to be the longest-lasting of his relationships. Despite the fact that the liaison did not come to the fruition Beethoven hoped for, Josephine provided him with an invaluable emotional anchor. This helped him cope with his withdrawal from society because of his deafness and with what he described as his 'miserable life'.

Private Collection, Germany/Malvisi Archives

Beethoven's friendship with the Malfattis (above) ended when his advances were rejected by Therese (seated at the piano). His close friend Ignaz von Gleichenstein was married to Anna Malfatti (playing the guitar). His doctor, Giovanni Malfatti (holding music) he next saw as he lay on his death-bed.

Beethoven took the cure at Bad Teplitz in the summers of 1811 and 1812. Here in 1812 he wrote two of the famous letters to the 'Immortal Beloved'.

Two of the women with whom Beethoven fell deeply in love: (top) Countess Giulietta Guicciardi and (above) Josephine von Brunsvik.

Many of the women Beethoven loved were at one time or another thought to have been the object of the feelings expressed in the letter to the 'Immortal Beloved'. However, Antonie Brentano (left), is the person to whom the letter was most likely written.

A wife in mind

In 1810, with some financial security behind him Beethoven seemed set on marriage. He even asked his friend Ignaz von Gleichenstein to look for a wife for him. It was with this end in mind that he pursued Therese Malfatti, the cousin of his doctor, Giovanni Malfatti, and sister of von Gleichenstein's fianceé.

Like Giulietta, Therese was very young – 18 to his 40 years – and beautiful. Beethoven even spruced up his appearance and asked his friend Dr. Wegeler in Bonn to find his baptismal certificate. However neither the lady in question nor her parents seemed very enthusiastic about the proposition, and he was rejected once again.

A brief friendship with Amalie Sebald, a singer, at Bad Teplitz, a spa town outside Vienna, in the summer of 1811 could well have developed further. However, so terrified was he of consummating this union of soul and body which was forever his ideal, that he excused himself from seeing her at Bad Teplitz the following year on account of illness.

This essential rejection of a love relationship is echoed in the letter to the 'Immortal Beloved', presumably never sent, found in Beethoven's desk after his death. Many books have been written on the subject of the possible recipient of this letter, which was written over a period of two days from July 6 1812 at Bad Teplitz. The strongest contender, Antonie Brentano, was put forward by Maynard Solomon in his Beethoven biography (1977). She was introduced to the composer by her sister-in-law Bettina Brentano, a flirtatious young woman who succeeded in charming both Beethoven and Goethe.

Antonie, who was Viennese, had married a Frankfurt businessman and moved with him to Frankfurt. Sadly, her health declined as she pined for her native city. Beethoven met her and her husband, Franz, while she was back in Vienna to be with her dying father and subsequently dealing with her father's estate. In all, she stayed three years, always delaying

Ferdinand Ries (above) a pupil and friend, was the son of Beethoven's violin teacher. With another friend, Franz Wegeler, he wrote a biography of Beethoven in 1838.

Stephan von Breuning (above) was a lifelong friend whom Beethoven met when they were both children in Bonn. In 1818 Anton Schindler (bottom), an Austrian law student and musician, joined Beethoven's circle. He published his **Biographie von Ludwig von Beethoven** *in 1840, but because he suppressed much original material it is not a totally reliable document.*

her return to Frankfurt. During this time Beethoven visited her often and played the piano to her for hours on end. A strong friendship which turned into a mutual love grew between them as one can surmise from the document to the 'Immortal Beloved'. This letter marked the moment of decision in the relationship. His confusion as he struggles to make up his mind is reflected in the letter:

While still abed my thoughts turn to you, my immortal beloved, some of them happy, some sad, waiting to see whether fate will hear us. I can live only completely with you or not at all... Your love makes me at once the happiest and unhappiest of men – at my age I need a certain uniform steadiness to my life – can this exist in our relationship?

Through this intense heartsearching Beethoven must have come face to face with what he had always known – that he could never settle down in a relationship. Thus, his last and greatest love paradoxically showed him that nothing really mattered to him as much as music and his independence. The mundane requirements of health, cleanliness, nourishment, comfort, sex and companionship were given low priority, and he must have known that no woman would have tolerated such conditions.

Friendships

Beethoven's friends were many and varied, and it is surprising in the light of his tempestuous nature that so many remained loyal to the end. He could be autocratic and domineering with outbursts of terrifying rage. Disagreements and reconciliations were an ordinary part of his life, and could be followed as quickly with excellent humour.

Several intimates from his Bonn years were important to him in Vienna. Stephan von Breuning was a lifelong friend, riding out the later storms with loyalty. Another from the Bonn circle was Count Waldstein who became one of his first patrons, recognizing Beethoven's importance at an early stage. There were also Franz Wegeler (later to marry Stephan's sister Eleonore) and Ferdinand Ries, son of his old violin teacher. Together they wrote a biography of the composer published in 1838. Beethoven generously gave Ries free piano lessons and encouraged him in his career as a composer.

Beethoven's temper was legendary, often aroused by imagined transgressions. The composer Hummel was commanded to 'Stay away! You are a false dog and the Devil take you.' The quarrel was made up with equal enthusiasm, Beethoven describing himself as 'a sour dumpling'. His broad humour, which delighted in puns, led him to write a piece to play with his friend Baron Zmeskall von Domanowecz entitled *Duet for Two Obbligato Eyeglasses* as both men required optical aid when sightreading music. However, although fond of playing practical jokes on others, Beethoven proved himself a 'sour dumpling' whenever jokes were played on him or when he was caught playing one. His friend, Ries, after hearing the newly-completed *Andante Favori* in the composer's apartment, called at Prince Lichnowsky's palace and wrote the piece down from memory. The next day the Prince visited Beethoven and played the music as if it were his own. Beethoven was baffled, then furious. Realizing what Ries had done he vowed that he would never play to him again, and apparently never did so.

His egalitarian streak demanded that the aristocracy be treated no more considerately than the friends of his own social station. One of his pupils, the young Archduke Rudolph experienced the indignity of rapped knuckles in reprisal for a mistake at the keyboard, yet he remained a faithful friend and patron until the composer's death. Prince Lobkowitz suffered the insult of being called an ass before his servants. He endured the composer's tantrums with great patience, and was rewarded with the dedications of the *Eroica, Fifth* and *Pastoral* Symphonies, plus several other major works. Few friendships survived without some sort of break or argument with the composer.

One very close friend whom Beethoven revered was the Baroness von Ertmann a celebrated pianist. He would write to her as 'My dear Dorothea Caecilia', equating her with the patron saint of music. She later recalled her friendship with Beethoven as one of 'unclouded friendship'. Probably much of the calmness of their association was due to her understanding how deafness was affecting him.

Towards the end of his life his friends fell into two main groups: one group centred round one of his publishers, Sigmund Anton Steiner and included

Michael Neder 'Scene in a Vienna Tavern' Historisches Museum der Stadt Wien/Erich Lessing/Magnum

Czerny and Schuppanzigh. The other group consisted of friends who gathered with him at favourite inns and restaurants and filled his conversation books with their questions and replies. Both sets were firmly under his control, indeed he saw himself as 'Generalissimo' of the Steiner group. The other set revered Beethoven as their 'master'. He was never slow to take advantage of adulation, dominating friends by sheer force of personality and making them into his willing slaves. He once remarked 'I value friends only by what they can do for me'. One such friend was Anton Schindler, a violinist and law student who moved into this circle around 1820. Apart from the inevitable furious disagreements he became his 'master's' unpaid companion, servant and amanuensis to the end of his life bearing insults ('A Miserable rogue, a derisory abject object') nobly. On Beethoven's death he appropriated a large collection of documents including the 400 conversation books two-thirds of which he destroyed in an attempt to whitewash the more unsavoury aspects of his hero's personality. Schindler's biography of Beethoven is therefore regarded as unreliable.

Dorothea von Ertmann (right), one of the most accomplished pianists in Vienna in Beethoven's time, was one of his close and enduring friends. To her he dedicated his Piano Sonata in A major, op. 101.

Beethoven frequently enjoyed spending his evenings out with friends. They usually gathered at favourite inns and restaurants such as the one illustrated here. Because of his deafness, his friends carried on their conversations with him in his Conversation Books, in which they wrote their questions, and also their replies to his own questions.

Beethoven sent this card (above) to Dorothea von Ertmann to celebrate New Year 1804. It reads: 'To Baroness Ertmann, For the New Year 1804, From her friend and admirer, Beethoven.'

Family

Members of his family were frequently a source of anguish to Beethoven. At the age of 16, after the death of his mother, he virtually became head of the family in the place of his alcoholic and spendthrift father, and this early acceptance of responsibility left an indelible mark. It was a sense of responsibility which was taken to extraordinary lengths. He felt it necessary to take a more than normal interest in the lives of his brothers and interfered where he saw fit.

His brothers Caspar Carl and Johann both came to Vienna in 1795. Johann went his own way, training to be an apothecary and eventually setting up a profitable business in Linz. Carl, possibly favoured more by Beethoven, was given much responsibility in the handling of the composer's business affairs. The manner in which he did this infuriated Beethoven's friends and associates. Not only did he sell works without Beethoven's knowledge as well as sell the same work to different publishers, but he became insufferably arrogant. Beethoven would react with fury and physical violence and then would be all-forgiving. But this blind love demanded a total loyalty in return. When Carl moved out of the shared lodgings with his brother in 1806 to marry Johanna Reiss, who was already pregnant, Beethoven responded immediately by cutting Carl out of his business affairs.

Six years later Johann also fell from grace. When Beethoven heard that he was having an affair with his housekeeper he took off for Linz in high moral dudgeon. However, Beethoven got the worst of the fisticuffs that followed and, either out of chivalry or anger, Johann married her immediately.

Carl van Beethoven died of tuberculosis in 1815. He left behind a will entrusting the guardianship of his only son Karl jointly to his wife and his brother Ludwig. His dying wish was for the two to 'be harmonious for the sake of my child's welfare' being well aware of the acrimony between Johanna and his brother.

Struggle for custody

There was however little harmony between these two in the ensuing years. By this time Beethoven had given up all thought of marriage, and immediately saw the role of guardian as one to which he could dedicate himself. He saw himself as the white knight who would rescue the unfortunate boy from the influence of his evil mother. This was the role in which he had cast Johanna from the first, for she had taken his brother away from him. Thus began five years of legal wrangling between Johanna and Beethoven over the possession of Karl. Beethoven eventually won custody of Karl, but not without numerous setbacks. He had no qualms about blackening Johanna's character, describing her as 'Queen of the Night' and vindictively dwelling at length on her unsuitability as a mother.

Rare visits from his mother, frequent changes of educational establishment and Beethoven's possessive demanding love for his 'son' would have seriously affected a weaker child than Karl. As he had behaved earlier towards his brothers so he behaved towards Karl. He wanted complete control over his destiny, even to the extent of forbidding him friends of his own age. After an initial two years boarding out at Giannatasio del Rio's school Karl lived with his uncle in chaotic squalour. It must have been hard for a bright young child to communicate with a deaf middle-aged uncle as well as embarrassing to be with him in public. Beethoven's behaviour became increasingly eccentric and indeed it was the general opinion in Vienna that he was half-crazy.

Although fond of his uncle, by 1826 the ten year strain of growing demands and continual reproaches became too much for Karl. In a deliberate act of defiance he tried to shoot himself near Baden, in an area where his uncle loved to walk. The attempt failed but it succeeded in freeing him from Beethoven's 'tormenting' influence. In a shocked state Beethoven agreed to his brother Johann's suggestion that Karl and he both stay in his country estate at Gneixendorf. They spent eight weeks here with Beethoven continuing to reproach Karl, even accusing him of having an affair with his aunt. When they eventually left for Vienna, Beethoven caught a nasty chill on the journey. Karl went into the army on his return, and wrote many solicitous letters to Beethoven as his health deteriorated. They were never to see each other again.

Beethoven was aware of his extraordinarily difficult personality and on one occasion begged a potential patron to 'judge me kindly and not to my disadvantage'. It was this complex nature that was both the source of and substance of his music. Despite his moods and difficult temperament, those closest to him felt his loss deeply. The poet Grillparzer perhaps best summed up the effect Beethoven's death had on his friends: 'It struck me like a sharp blow in my stomach, the tears sprang to my eyes'.

Beethoven's adversary in the battle for sole custody of his nephew, was Johanna, the boy's mother. He saw it as his mission to rescue the boy from the woman he likened to a character in Mozart's opera, **The Magic Flute.** *To him she represented the evil embodied in the 'Queen of the Night' (below).*

Archiv für Kunst und Geschichte

Erich Lessing/Magnum

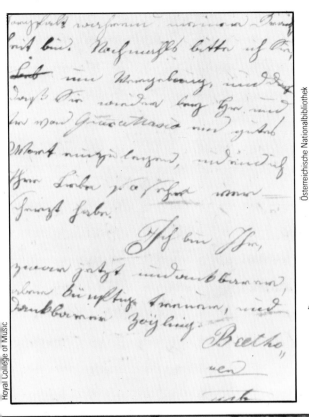

Karl von Beethoven (above), the nephew for whose sole custody Beethoven battled for many years. A letter (left) written by Karl to one of the daughters of his schoolmaster, apologizing for his bad behaviour. In it he promises to be good and asks the young lady to put in a good word for him with his schoolmaster.

Johann, Beethoven's youngest brother (above). He fell from favour when he married. He was an apothecary in Linz and later became a landowner at Gneixendorf, near Krems.

The music room in Johann's house in Gneixendorf. Beethoven and Karl spent eight weeks here after Karl's attempted suicide. Although the visit was at the invitation of Johann, it is known that he charged Beethoven rent for the stay. On the return journey to Vienna Beethoven became ill.

COMPOSER'S LIFE

The artist and his patrons

Most 18th-century composers were dependent upon – some to the extent of being employed by – wealthy aristocratic patrons. Beethoven was a freelance but, especially after deafness forced him to give up his career as a pianist, he still needed patrons. The relationship was, however, always on his terms. He considered himself the superior of any aristocrat and would never pander to his patrons' whims, as 18th-century composers had had to do. Most patrons forgave him because they admired his greatness and some undoubtedly wanted to bask in his reflected glory. By the end of his life Beethoven's income was increasingly derived from public performances supported by the rising middle classes. This trend continued and successful modern composers no longer owe their living to powerful aristocrats, but to the concert-going and music-buying public.

'There is only one Beethoven'

Throughout his life, Beethoven was sustained by the generous support of wealthy patrons – they, in turn, basked in his reflected glory. But the high-minded composer was never an easy man to patronize.

Prince, what you are, you are by an accident of birth; what I am, I am through myself. There have been, and will still be, thousands of princes. There is only one Beethoven.' Thus wrote the 35-year-old composer to Prince Karl Lichnowsky, the first and foremost of his Viennese patrons.

It was a remarkable outburst. Only Beethoven could have made it. Few composers then could earn enough to support themselves independently and nearly all relied heavily upon the goodwill of wealthy patrons. To upset a patron was to risk your very livelihood.

But Beethoven was a proud man, deeply conscious of the dignity of his own calling, and he resented the need to ingratiate himself with patrons – most of whom were in his eyes, morally and intellectually inferior. What he wanted, more than anything, was the freedom to compose – to be at someone's beck and call, an evening's entertainment for his patron's friends, was to stop him creating music.

The letter to Lichnowsky was prompted by just the kind of incident that Beethoven must have disliked most – but the kind of situation that other patronized composers had accepted for years.

Lichnowsky was actually one of Beethoven's most understanding and generous patrons, and the two had known each other for years when, in October 1806, the composer was a guest at Lichnowsky's beautiful hilltop castle of Grätz in Silesia. At the time, the French army of Napoleon was still occupying this part of Europe, after conquering the Austrians and Russians at Austerlitz. But Prince Lichnowsky, now the battles were a year past, saw no reason not to invite a French general and some of his officers, together with other guests, to a musical soirée at which Beethoven would play some of his recent compositions.

Unfortunately for the music-loving and hospitable Prince, the composer declared stubbornly that he would not perform. Hoping still to be able to persuade him to do so when the time came, the Prince let the planned evening go ahead. Perhaps, after 14 years' acquaintance, he should have known Beethoven better.

The grand dinner at the castle went smoothly enough, but Beethoven was glowering and unsociable. After dinner the company assembled expectantly in the big music-room. But Beethoven

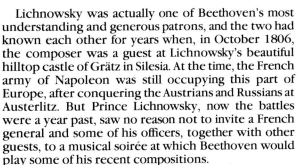

Prince Karl Lichnowsky, pictured (above left) was one of Beethoven's most devoted and long-suffering friends as well as a very active and generous supporter. Beethoven, who was both touchy and demanding in his relationship with his patrons, is shown in the painting above.

Grätz castle (below), where Beethoven received generous hospitality, was the country home of his patron Prince Lichnowsky.

Edimedia

Frau von Breuning, widow of a court councillor and her family, seen in the silbouette above, provided a second home for Beethoven while he lived in Bonn. He gave piano lessons to two of her four children and through the wide circle of intellectual friends he met at the house, he became familiar with the literary and philosophical ideas of the day.

stormed off to his room, packed his belongings, and without a further word strode out of the castle and into the pouring rain. He walked to the house of a doctor friend in the nearest town, where he spent the night before continuing by coach to Vienna.

It was on this rain-soaked walk, some people believe, that the manuscript of Beethoven's 'Appassionata' Sonata for piano was badly stained by water. The composer caught a nasty chill as well, to add to his woes.

The letter to Prince Lichnowsky was written almost immediately afterwards, it seems. And Beethoven's temper had not abated by the time he reached his lodgings in Vienna. He took the bust of his patron and friend which stood on a cabinet in his workroom and smashed it on the floor.

Family tradition

Beethoven, like many composers before him, needed patrons. Yet he did his best to ensure that the patronage was on his terms. He also had a great deal of music published – unlike Schubert – and often wrote to commission. Indeed, Beethoven has been described as 'the first great freelance composer'.

There is no doubt that Beethoven's famil background must have helped him towards th independent attitude. His grandfather and father wer both professional musicians at the Electoral Court a Bonn. His grandfather Ludwig, the son of a bake became a church organist and choirmaster in hi native town, Le Mechelin (now Malines in Belgium while he was still in his teens. At the age of 21, in 173 he joined the Bonn Court Chapel as a singer – his quit high salary (400 Florins) suggested that he was gifte as does his steady rise to the chief musical post c Kapellmeister in 1761.

Ludwig's son, Johann van Beethoven, born in 174C quite naturally took to music and entered the Cour Chapel as a treble chorister. Under his father' instruction he had also learned the clavier (keyboard and could play the violin. In 1764, he too was taken o the Court payroll at an annual salary of 100 Florins - far less than his father's starting salary, but it may hav been a part-time post. Either way, Johann earne enough to marry in 1767. His first child died i infancy; the second, born in 1770, was the futur composer.

Beethoven never really knew his grandfather, who died when he was two. But the tradition o professional musicianship was undoubtedly passe on. In 1781, Beethoven, aged ten, was already assistin his teacher Neefe as organist at some lesser services i the Bonn Court Chapel. Little over a year later, he wa earning a Court salary of 150 Florins as an organist an orchestral harpsichord player. So, at the age of 20, h already had a good salaried income, just as had hi grandfather and father. He had enough to live on an his rapidly developing talent was fully recognized. Ye Beethoven was unsettled.

This was a strange society for an ambitious an intellectual young man to grow up in, one which wa beginning uneasily to come to terms with th enormous cultural shock of the French Revolution i

Three generations of Beethovens were employed at the court of the Elector of Cologne which had its seat at Bonn (far right). Beethoven's grandfather (right) was a talented and successful musician who became Kapellmeister at the Bonn Court chapel. His father sang as a tenor while Beethoven himself played viola in the court orchestra from an early age.

Beethoven-Haus Bonn/Lauros-Giraudon

89 – the year the Bastille was stormed.

Since about 1784 the young musician had been on qual social terms with the aristocratic von Breuning mily as their 'music teacher' and friend – he even ught the Austrian ambassador the piano. He became iendly too with Count Waldstein, eight years his nior. Intellectually he was, in the company of such eople, awakening to classic and romantic literature cluding Goethe's *Sorrows of young Werther*.

A visit to Vienna in 1787, supported it seems by the ector of Bonn, enabled him to meet Mozart and to ay to him. He would have known nothing of Mozart's nancial troubles and would have seen only the great, nd above all, independent, artist at work. When aydn passed through Bonn, too, Beethoven would ave seen only the international traveller and elebrated musician and perhaps have forgotten the) years' Esterházy service during which Haydn had owly built his reputation.

ennese princes

hen Beethoven, aged 21, finally left Bonn in 1792 for new home in Vienna, though, it was the war with ance (which was now uncomfortably close) as well his ambition that drove him. The Elector seems nce again to have helped with travel expenses, and is Bonn salary continued for a while. He intended to ke composition lessons from Haydn, and in the eantime he found lodgings, first in an unidentified tic room and then on the ground floor of No 45 lser Gasse. One other occupant of this latter house as Prince Lichnowsky. Lichnowsky and his wife rincess Christiane, both of whom were intellectual nd passionately musical, then actually took eethoven into their own luxurious apartments, here he stayed until 1795 – two years and more.

In 1794 Beethoven's Bonn grant dried up but Prince ichnowsky stepped generously into the breach. He aid him 600 Thalers – a very good salary indeed –

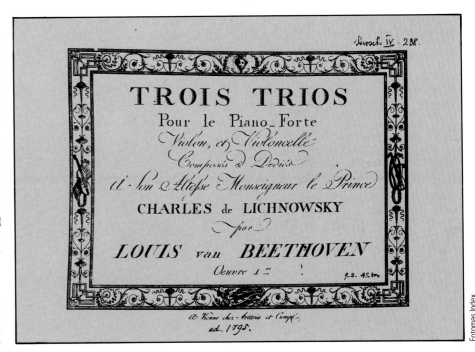

until he should find 'a suitable post', and also paid for the cost of publishing his three piano trios, Op 1. His wholly unselfish aim was evidently that the young musical genius should have every opportunity to fulfil himself, and when he visited Beethoven in his workroom he was far too respectful of 'the Muse' to interrupt. According to a friend:

They agreed that neither was to notice the other's presence, so that the master would not be disturbed. The Prince would say, 'Good morning', look through a manuscript, watch the master working for a bit and then leave with a friendly 'Adieu'. Even so

One way in which Beethoven could express his appreciation to his patrons and remain on equal terms was by dedicating his works to them. Above is the title page to the piano trios which he dedicated to his friend and patron Prince Lichnowsky.

Beethoven conducts a piano quintet (right) at the home of his celebrated patron, Count Razumovsky. The count (below right) was not only a music lover but also a capable violinist. As Russian ambassador in Vienna from 1792 almost continuously until his death in 1836 he did much to encourage the arts and sciences.

Österreichische Nationalbibliothek

these visits disturbed Beethoven, who sometimes locked the door. Without taking umbrage, the Prince would walk down the three flights of stairs . . . and wait until the door opened and he could offer a friendly greeting to the Prince of Music.

Lichnowksy was by no means Beethoven's only patron in these early Viennese years. There was Baron Nikolaus Zmeskall von Domanovecz, a vineyard proprietor from Hungary, who arranged chamber concerts in his home so that the young composer could present his works to the 'right people'. Beethoven liked the company of Zmeskall on a walk or over a meal at their favourite restaurant, the White Swan, but teased the nobleman with nicknames like 'food-gulper' or 'Baron Muckdriver'.

The Russian Count Razumovsky, ambassador of his country in Vienna, also provided a great deal of help. Razumovsky, who was related to the Lichnowskys, was an expert violinist who liked playing in quartets and was quite capable of joining the professionals of the Schuppanzigh Quartet (which he supported financially) in music by Haydn, Mozart or Beethoven. It was to him that the composer dedicated the three 'Razumovsky' Quartets of 1805–6. He knew and admired Beethoven for some 20 years. According to one contemporary the Schuppanzigh Quartet was put completely at Beethoven's disposal in the Count's spacious music room. Everything Beethoven wrote for this type of ensemble could be tried out instantly and, it seemed to Beethoven, that every note was played just as he wanted it played, 'with such devotion, such love, such obedience, such piety as could only be inspired by passionate admiration of his great genius.'

There were other patrons, too, wealthy and usually titled people who clearly felt privileged to help a genius to cope with the sheer necessities of life. Baron Gottfried van Swieten, considered a great arbiter of Viennese musical taste, was another sponsor of concerts who gave his support. Beethoven rewarded him with the dedication of his First Symphony. Count Johann Georg von Camus, in the dedication of some string trios (Op. 9) was described by the composer as 'the first Maecenas of his Muse'.

Historisches Museum, Vienna

It was von Camus who, in a moment of great generosity, once gave Beethoven his horse.

The contract of 1809

Beethoven could attend to all musical matters. Practical help was what he needed, and he received it in abundance: lodging, concert 'exposure' of his works, actual gifts of money and concert fees, a supply of well-to-do pupils, subscriptions towards the publication of a new piece, and so on. Friedrich Wilhelm II, the King of Prussia, gave him a gold snuffbox filled with louis d'or: perhaps a royal pun on his name (Ludwig was 'Louis' in French). And yet he seems always to have felt somewhat insecure.

His growing deafness threatened his career as a pianist, certainly, and doubtless this contributed to his unease. Once, in Prince Lobkowitz's house, he fell into

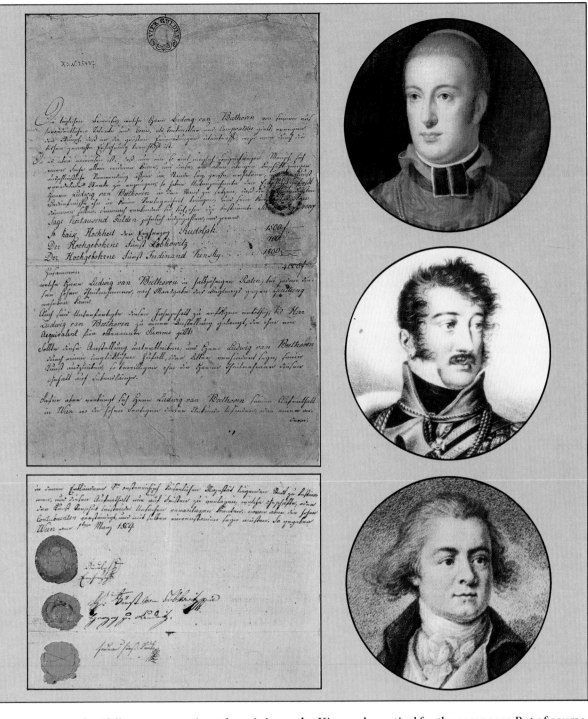

On March 10 1809 three of Beethoven's most loyal patrons – Archduke Rudolph, Prince Kinsky and Prince Lobkowitz (top to bottom) signed a contract (left) guaranteeing the composer a salary of 4000 Florins a year for life. In return Beethoven agreed to stay in Vienna. Needless to say, the contract was not honoured to the letter.

conversation with a fellow guest, and confessed that he:

wished to be relieved from having to negotiate the sale of his works, and would gladly find someone willing to pay him a certain income for life, for which he should possess the exclusive right of publishing all he wrote.

This actually came about, more or less, in March 1809. Beethoven had had an offer from the King of Westphalia – Napoleon's younger brother Jerome Bonaparte – to join his Court as First Kapellmeister. The salary was high and the conditions of work undemanding. In fact both the King and Beethoven seem to have conceived of the post as largely a prestige one with benefits on both sides, cultural for

the King and practical for the composer. But of course, it would mean leaving Vienna where he was greatly valued – and where he was probably happy to stay. Nevertheless, Beethoven accepted the offer, at least in principle, presumably to put pressure on his Viennese patrons to come up with a matching offer. They reacted swiftly. Would a regular income retain Beethoven in Vienna, where he was so much valued? Hurried negotiations began, and the composer laid down his conditions:

Beethoven has so great a predilection for life in this city, so much gratitude for the proofs of good will which he has received here, and so much patriotism for his second fatherland, that he . . . will never make his domicile elsewhere if the opportunities . . . are measurably offered him here . . . Beethoven should receive from a great personage assurance of a salary for life; even a number of persons of high rank might contribute to the sum. This salary, under the existing conditions of high cost of living, could not be less than 4000 Florins a year.

Matters were soon arranged. On 1 March 1809, three patrons agreed to pay Beethoven the 4000 Florins, in half-yearly instalments. Archduke Rudolph was to contribute Fl 1500, Prince Lobkowitz Fl 700, and Prince Ferdinand Kinsky Fl 1800. Archduke Rudolph, at this time aged only 21, was the composer's pupil and friend – it was to him that Beethoven later dedicated the 'Archduke' Piano Trio and the *Missa Solemnis,* masterpieces of chamber music and choral music respectively. Prince Kinsky is a slightly more shadowy figure, and it seems that Beethoven did not actually know him personally at the time of the 1809 contract, though he met him afterwards.

Unfortunately, the apparently watertight contract became suspect with the passage of the next few years. Spiralling inflation ate into the real value of the salary. And, by 1816, both Prince Kinsky and Lobkowitz had died. Their estates continued to pay Beethoven, rather less regularly, and the Kinsky family reduced their payments by Fl 600.

Furthermore the world of the wealthy aristocratic landowners was changing slowly and inexorably, as were their hitherto secure finances. Beethoven continued to press Lobkowitz (in 1813 even going to law about it) for an increase in his contribution to counter inflation, but the Prince was in serious financial trouble himself. Count Razumovsky's palace burnt down, with the loss of many treasures, and he

Historisches Museum, Vienna

The last of Beethoven's many apartments (above) was described by one appalled eye-witness as: 'Everything mixed together, scores, shirts, socks, books It was to this chaos that his patrons were invited.

Archiv für Kunst und Geschichte

The first really professional composer, Beethoven developed a significant business relationship with his publishers, Ataria & Co., who published all his works with opus numbers 1–8. They occupied premises in the Kohlmarkt in Vienna (foreground right of picture).

Historisches Museum, Vienna

oo had to make economies. One of Beethoven's ldest friends and earliest supporters, Count Valdstein, sank terribly into debt and, when he died in 823, he was in such poverty that the doctors' bills ould not be paid, and a friend had to find the money or a funeral.

But as the aristocracy declined, so the middle and rofessional classes rose to take their place in upporting composers. Beethoven's published music ncreased and musical societies began to take a more nd more significant role in fostering his, and many ther composers' music.

By the time Beethoven died in 1827, the age of the wealthy patron with an ensemble of domestic musicians was on the wane. The aristocracy continued to patronize music – Wagner could hardly have managed without King Ludwig of Bavaria – but performances moved more and more into the public domain, and the income from these performances was often enough to support the more successful composers. Beethoven might have been pleased, but there is no doubt that the generosity of patrons like Lichnowsky and Razumovsky helped Beethoven to let his 'divine fire' burn.

By 1795 Beethoven was in huge demand. He achieved great prestige when he was commissioned to compose two sets of dances for the annual masked ball held in the Redoutensaal (left) in the Hofburg palace.

COMPOSER'S LIFE

An enduring musical legacy

Beethoven was one of the greatest innovators in the history of music. In the 18th century, music had been considered a lesser art than painting and literature. Beethoven's achievement was to so raise the status of music, especially instrumental music, that the English critic Walter Pater could write that 'all arts aspire to the condition of music'. Like other revolutionary artists, Beethoven influenced not only his contemporaries but also subsequent composers, Brahms being the best-known example. Modern composers are still indebted to Beethoven and not just because of his musical legacy. After Beethoven it was impossible for anyone to regard a composer as a mere journeyman; in Denis Arnold's words, 'The great composer is now appreciated as a man worthy of great respect and even the less able may be regarded as men of skill and integrity.'

'He freed music'

Beethoven was the archetypal Romantic arti
Scarcely any significant composer since his d
has escaped his influence or failed to
acknowledge the continuing power of his wo

Beethoven caught the popular imagination to an extent that was quite unprecedented for a composer. In the age of Romanticism, his ability to grip an audience with the sheer power of emotion in his music, together with the intensely romantic image of the man himself, elevated him to the status of hero. Yet, as we know, he was no fleeting idol, here one moment and forgotten the next, for the technical leaps forward that he made in his music influenced the composers that were to follow him for more than 100 years.

Beethoven's last years coincided with a broadening of musical audiences; no longer based on narrow aristocratic circles they now became bigger, more middle-class and more demonstrative. Beethoven's music reflected a spirit of social equality and heroism that was in keeping with the great political upsurges of his day, and these new audiences readily identified with his message. Despite Beethoven's audacious handling of music as it had previously existed, his first audiences were deeply affected, even enthusiastic. It is remarkable that nearly all Beethoven's major concert works – the symphonies, the concertos, the greatest of the piano sonatas and the chamber works – entered the standard repertoire from the first and each has stayed there.

But Beethoven's immediate and enduring status, among both musicians and music-lovers, was due to much more than the sheer power and excitement of his work. From the beginning people read into Beethoven's work some of the struggles that had marked his life. Fed by an ever-growing army of biographers and 'myth-makers', Beethoven's audiences (and imitators) eagerly interpreted the noble qualities that had influenced their hero's achievements: his brave struggle against deafness, his disappointments in love and his intense devotion to his work. Mindful of their subject's appeal as a 'man of the people', many of these biographers ignored aspects of Beethoven's personality – his fondness for the aristocratic 'van' of his name, for example – that might have contradicted his popular image. Even the names bestowed by the composer and by others to his works – the *Eroica* Symphony, the *Pathétique* Sonata, the *Appassionata* Sonata and the *Emperor* Concerto – attracted a certain air of reverence. Not

surprisingly Germany, the country of his birth, and Vienna, the city of his adoption, both laid claim to Beethoven's unique greatness. In 1870, the centenary of his birth, the house where he was born in Bonn was made into a proud national shrine but, not to be outdone, the Viennese responded in 1900 by unveiling the most grandiose of the many monuments that have been raised in his honour.

Beethoven's inheritance

Beethoven was a great innovator in that he used the music of the 18th century in such a way that it was transformed and shaken free from any restraints of form. In this he took advantage of the great technical changes in the science of music that were taking place during his lifetime. For much of his career Beethoven had to contend with severe limitations in what instruments could do, and he contributed in some measure towards their advancement. For example, he had a fierce desire to see improvements made in the pianoforte and he followed develop-

Included in Beethoven's musical inheritance was the 18th-century orchestra, which had been established more or less in its present form by a group of composers working at the Elector's Court at Mannheim. One of the founders of this 'Mannheim School' was the German composer and musician, Franz Xaver Richter (above). He is portrayed conducting with a furled manuscript.

Christoph Willibald von Gluck (left) was an influential 18th-century German composer who made an important contribution to the history of music by striking a new balance between music and drama in opera. From Gluck onwards, composers – and Beethoven is a supreme example – tried to inject their work with more dramatic content.

J. L. David · Napoleon Crossing the Alps · Malmaison/Bulloz

Revolution, war, empire: these dramatic words were on the lips of Beethoven's contemporaries as Napoleon (left) marched through Europe. And just as the French emperor dominated politics as the 'liberator' who would usher in a new age of democracy, so Beethoven was hailed as the 'man who freed music'.

C. P. E. Bach (below) was the second surviving son of the great J. S. Bach. He was one of the first composers to realize the essential qualities of the piano, qualities Beethoven was to develop enormously.

Mansell Collection

ments in piano-making avidly.

The symphony orchestra, which had been established more or less in its modern form by a group of composers working at the Elector's court at Mannheim around the middle of the 18th century, was still relatively new when Beethoven came to it. Previously, an orchestra had comprised a string band with a harpsichord and any other instruments that happened to be available. But the Mannheim musicians regularized the wind section as two flutes and/or oboes, two horns and/or trumpets with timpani, two bassoons and, sometimes, two clarinets.

Through his symphonies Beethoven further enlarged this basic 18th-century orchestra. He standardized the clarinets, added another horn or two and, in a dramatic gesture, introduced piccolo, double bassoon and three trombones into the last movement of his Fifth Symphony. At a stroke, therefore, he added brilliance at the top end, depth at the bottom and powerful richness in the middle. In these circumstances the presence of a keyboard instrument in the orchestra became unnecessary, so that it reappeared with the orchestra only when used as a solo instrument. Beethoven was especially responsive to the piano's potential as a solo element, and the orchestra he helped create still serves as a basic model for most modern composers.

Storm and stress

The great composers of the 18th century brought music to a finely-polished sophistication. Christoph Willibald von Gluck had changed the operatic

Begun during his lifetime, Beethoven's 'canonization' really took off after his death as busts, portraits, biographies and statues commemorated the great artist. In 1845 funds for the Bonn statue (above right) fell short, but Liszt (above) came to the rescue with the proceeds from six triumphant concerts.

hearted side of the music with a menacing and disturbing side.

For the artists of this movement art, in order to reflect truth, had to reflect the tragedy of life. During the 1780s and 1790s this sombre outlook was showing signs of staleness. Aware of this, a number of composers attempted to resuscitate the art of music by bold and sometimes bizarre experiments, but a new and vital figure was needed to breathe fire into the old forms so that they might support further development. Beethoven was that figure. His fresh approach increased both content and expression far beyond anything his predecessors and contemporaries could have imagined. Not only did he rescue music handsomely from its threatened torpor, but he injected it with totally new and dynamic life that raised it onto a higher plateau of development and prepared it for a continuing evolution that endures to this day.

overture from a brilliant but empty-headed prelude into a symphonic statement, which was designed to prepare the mood of the audience for the drama to follow. Carl Philipp Emanuel Bach had greatly deepened the emotional content of music in his keyboard sonatas and, together with Haydn and Mozart, had developed orchestral writing to a rare state of perfection. These and many other composers had at times adopted a dark and ominous style of music called *Sturm und Drang* (Storm and Stress; a name and an artistic mood borrowed from German literature) which supplemented the joyous, light-

Beethoven's innovations

Music, just as much as any other human endeavour, needs rules. In his early years, while he was still learning his art, Beethoven was fond of questioning the rules of music whenever they were explained to him. Why, he asked, should a movement be constructed in such a manner? Why must one always compose for certain instruments in certain ways? Why is it wrong to write some combinations of notes? Later, after he had broken many of these rules

An amusing silhouette (left) shows Bruckner taking snuff from Wagner. Both these composers, who were far from modest about their own achievements, cited Beethoven as a mentor. Wagner even said that his own art took up at the point where Beethoven's had left off, while Bruckner allegedly claimed that he was the only composer he knew who could measure up to Beethoven.

and still encountered success, an academic pointed out to him that it was not allowed to write a certain harmony that appeared in one of his scores. 'Then I permit it', retorted Beethoven, thus closing the matter.

Beethoven's way of 'permitting' rules to be broken is in fact one of the measures of his genius. In the Piano Concerto no. 4, for example, the pianist announces the melody (in direct defiance of a tradition which stated that the orchestra always makes a lengthy statement before the soloist enters). In Symphony no. 3, after two sharp 'Attention!' chords, the main theme is announced on cellos, rather than the conventional violins, and is immediately contradicted by disruptive violin syncopations. And the Violin Concerto begins, of all things, with a solo drum. There are countless other examples of originality throughout Beethoven's music, but in breaking the rules he was not simply being rebellious for he built a new music upon the foundations of the old.

Expanding the scale

Beethoven's concept of scale was also new. There had been long works before – Bach's monumental oratorios, for example, and the great Masses of Haydn and Mozart – but no previous composer expanded the time scale of music as consistently as Beethoven did. His *Eroica* Symphony, for instance, is about half as long again as any previous symphony, and these heroic proportions are encountered in every aspect of his instrumental music: from concerto, overture, sonata through to quartet and variations. But Beethoven was never an innovator for innovation's sake. There is no evidence of padding in his music: every note makes an essential contribution to the whole, and this results in an incredible concentration of thought. Beethoven's sketchbooks reveal how he struggled with themes and phrases.

Beethoven's influence is clearly audible in the work of his successors. An understanding of his pioneering work leads to a finer appreciation of many of the works of 20th-century masters such as Béla Bartók (below) and Ralph Vaughan Williams (right).

Mansell Collection

The power of Beethoven's music to evoke profound emotions among listeners is captured in this 19th-century Italian painting of a recital (below).

By Courtesy of the National Portrait Gallery, London

Sometimes he worked on them for years, rejecting a note here, remodelling a phrase there, and slowly hammering them into shape until he was sure he had achieved the maximum effect with the minimum of notes. While some of Beethoven's works are no longer than those of Mozart or Haydn, they are so full of feeling and intensity that they seem longer and greater in content.

Symphonic unity

There is, however, also a feeling of profound satisfaction, brought about by another of Beethoven's composing secrets. In all of his large-scale works he used his melodies with the utmost economy. Once he had settled upon a phrase or melody, he would squeeze every last ounce of meaning from it: by letting it evolve, combine with itself, join with other themes, become splintered and reunited, and, on occasion, change into something apparently unconnected with the original so that the music grows and develops like a natural being. Beethoven liked to play with words in his conversations and letters, and was just as much a master of puns in his music. As a result listeners experience a feeling that the music has a satisfying sense of unity and continuity. Perhaps this is why audiences find Beethoven's music so accessible.

'A crass monster'

From the start audiences took to Beethoven's concert music. They recognized its 'logic' without having any idea as to how it had been achieved, its greatness being evident but inexplicable. It was left to the professional music critics to do the explaining, but since they did not share Beethoven's genius or breadth of vision they were unable to write with complete understanding about the music. As one London critic wrote of Beethoven's compositions: 'most of what he produces is . . . so full of unaccountable and often repulsive harmonies, that he puzzles the critic as much as he perplexes the

Civico Museo Revoltella, Trieste/Scala

performer'. And in 1804 a Viennese critic summed up the sunny Sympony no. 2 in the following manner:

. . . a crass monster, a hideously writhing wounded dragon, that refuses to expire, and though bleeding in the Finale, furiously beats about with its tail erect,

In 1829 another critic wrote of the *Eroica* Symphony that it was 'infinitely too lengthy'. 'If this symphony is not by some means abridged', he continued, 'it will soon fall into disuse.'

Four years earlier another London writer found the vast power of the Symphony no. 9 ('Choral') altogether too much for him. '[It] made even the very ground shake under us.' That critic, however, acknowledged that this was what the audiences wanted, for he went on: 'Beethoven finds from all public accounts, that noisy extravagance of execution and outrageous clamour in musical performance more frequently ensures applause than chastened elegance or refined judgement.'

Even composers found Beethoven's music indigestible. On hearing the first movement of the Seventh Symphony, Weber pronounced that Beethoven was 'now ripe for the madhouse'; while Louis Spohr admitted in his autobiography that Beethoven's last works, including the titanic Symphony no. 9, gave him no enjoyment. 'Beethoven', he wrote in refined and carefully worded sorrow, 'was deficient in aesthetic imagery and lacked a sense of beauty.' But it was not only the symphonies which came under fire from those who should have known better. A French writer announced that Beethoven's last piano sonata displayed 'the madness of genius'.

The early biographers, perhaps conscious that their hero's popularity was destined to endure for decades, even centuries, were less ready to condemn any part of his music. Some gave it their uncritical blanket approval; others – the more daring among them – attempted detailed appraisal, often admitting defeat over the 'meaning' of the last sonatas and quartets. Even today some writers believe that those mysterious late works, written while the composer endured the misery of total deafness, are still only slowly giving up their secrets. That is another reason for the continuing mystique which surrounds the composer and his music, for after a century and a half there remain profundities to be explored.

Beethoven's unmistakable voice

It was inevitable that Beethoven's music should influence his contemporaries and successors. Not only did he serve them by providing new formal conventions, but the depth of his feeling, the vastness of his designs, and the apparent spirituality which surrounded his composing have all encouraged later composers to emulate him.

Schubert's delicate and Romantic art grew out of Mozart's Classical perfection yet gained subtly from his study of Beethoven's music. Even Beethoven's style of playing the piano, with its emphasis on musical content rather than playing technique, finds an echo in Schubert. It was a style which largely lapsed until the late piano works of Brahms, although the sincere if slightly ostentatious sonatas of Schumann should not be overlooked. (Only in the present century, with the piano works of Scriabin, Busoni and Nielsen, can this line of development be seen to have made further substantial advances.)

It was due largely to his examination of Beethoven's orchestral works that Schumann embarked on his own series of four symphonies. The

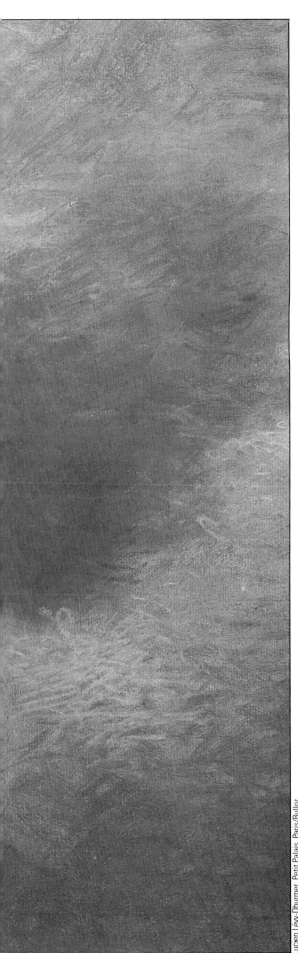

unmistakable voice of Beethoven will be heard, for example, in the slow movement of Schumann's Symphony no. 2, just as the cyclic principle (the appearance of identical or closely-related themes in two or more movements) in Schumann's Fourth and Brahms's Third Symphonies may be traced directly to Beethoven's Fifth.

The slow movement (*Scène aux champs* — Scene in the Country) of Berlioz's *Symphonie Fantastique* may well have been different if he had not had the example of Beethoven's Symphony no. 6 (*Pastoral*) to draw upon; and the opening of Berlioz's *King Lear* Overture owes a debt to the lower strings' recitative section (in which speech rhythms are imitated) in the last movement of the 'Choral' Symphony.

Brahms's indebtedness to Beethoven is well known: the composer himself freely admitted it. When a critic pointed out the similarity between the main themes in the last movements of Brahms's First Symphony and Beethoven's Ninth, Brahms snapped: 'Any fool can see that!' The ghostly rhythmic link between the scherzo and finale of Beethoven's Fifth Symphony clearly served as a model for a similar link in Vaughan Williams's Fourth Symphony, and when Beethoven transferred the headlong Scherzo from chamber music to the symphony, replacing the stately traditional minuet, he started a convention that continues unabated to this day.

Béla Bartók's string quartets, some of the most formidable music of the 20th century, are more easily understood by audiences familiar with Hungarian folk music. Equally those who know Beethoven's late quartets are likely to gain a fuller appreciation of Bartók's. Dvořák and Bruckner were clearly indebted to Beethoven while Wagner, thoroughly uninhibited by modesty, openly declared that his art took up at the point Beethoven's left off. Sibelius took Beethoven's concentration of phrase and melody to its logical conclusion, and many modern composers acknowledge their debt to him, showing that the influence of his music still exerts a powerful effect.

One of them, the English composer Robert Simpson, readily notes his debt to both Haydn and Beethoven in his employment of 'organic structure – the feel of creating current, creating movement'. Simpson's studies of Beethoven's compositional processes have led him to write three string quartets, nos. 4, 5 and 6, which 'constitute a close study of Beethoven's *Razumovsky* Quartets (op. 59, nos. 1–3) with the aim of enhancing understanding of them even if it be at the expense of my own'.

Beethoven's everlasting popularity

Probably because of his advanced musical thinking, which puzzled and intrigued his listeners, and his almost superhuman struggle with and eventual triumph over his deafness, people of the 19th century saw Beethoven as epitomizing the popular romantic image of the artist as hero. He conquered great hardship in order to produce for the enjoyment of the world works of art apparently conceived as the result of a spiritual union with God. This image continues to the present day. Despite attempts by some critics to deflate the 'Beethoven myth', his popularity now is greater than ever.

In the 20th century massive media exposure in the form of books, articles, concerts and recordings have kept Beethoven's name firmly before the music-loving public, and the notable success of these extensive projects shows that his music still exerts a powerful influence on musicians and listeners alike.

Even while he was alive, Beethoven's ruggedly uncompromising features, and his unmistakably stubborn posture (below), attracted artists. But after his death he was virtually deified in paintings that idealized him as the ultimate tortured Romantic, whose indomitable spirit triumphed over impossible odds (left).

Contemporary composers

Carl Czerny (1791-1857)

Born in Vienna the son of a musician, Czerny was a pupil of Beethoven from 1800 to 1803 and earned a reputation as one of his finest interpreters. From 1816 to 1823, he held weekly concerts devoted to Beethoven's music at his parents' home. Known chiefly as a teacher – Liszt was one of his pupils – he also composed and published over a thousand works, including symphonies, overtures, songs and concertos. He died in Vienna in 1857.

Johann Hummel (1778-1837)

Born in Pressburg (now Bratislava, Czechoslovakia), Hummel became a pupil of Mozart in 1786 in Vienna. His father, also a musician, took him on an extended concert tour in 1788 and in 1793 he returned to Vienna to study with Salieri and Haydn. He became a friend and rival of Beethoven, but spent much of his working life out of Vienna – as Konzertmeister to Prince Esterhazy for seven years, as Kapellmeister at Weimar and then Stuttgart, or on tour. Best remembered as a pianist and teacher, he wrote much music, including several ballets, but no symphonies. He died at Weimar in 1837.

Anton Reicha (1770-1836)

Born in Prague, Czechoslovakia, Reicha was first taught by his uncle, the cellist Josef Reicha. On a visit to Bonn in 1805, he made friends with Beethoven and then settled in Vienna for some years before moving permanently to Paris in 1808. There he composed and wrote treatises, which gained him a professorship at the Paris Conservatoire in 1818. Among his pupils were Liszt, Berlioz and Cesar Frank, who valued his teaching for its precision and open-mindedness. In 1831 he was awarded the Legion d'Honneur, having become a French citizen. His best known compositions are the *36 Fugues* of 1803, dedicated to Haydn, and his *Wind Quintets*.

Gioacchino Rossini (1792-1868)

Rossini was born in Pesaro on the Adriatic, the son of a trumpeter. Exceptionally precocious – he was admitted to the Philharmonic Academy of Bologna at the age of 12 – he had immense success with his first two operas in Venice in 1813: *Tancredi* and *The Italian Girl in Algiers*. In 1815 he became musical director of the San Carlo and Fonda theatres in Naples, where he wrote many of his most famous operas – *The Barber of Seville, Cinderella, Othello* and *Moses in Egypt* – all characterized by an exuberant energy. In Paris from 1824 to 1830, he wrote the grand opera *William Tell*, returning to Italy to write his *Stabat Mater* in 1831, before lapsing into years of unproductive depression. Finally he returned to Paris, to enjoy an Indian summer of happiness and composition, dying there after writing the *Petite Messe Sonelle*. Today he is best known for his comic operas.

Louis Spohr (1784-1859)

Spohr, the eldest son of a doctor who was an amateur flautist, was born in Brunswick, Germany. In his early years he toured through Europe with immense success as a virtuoso violinist. In England he caused a sensation in 1820 by conducting the London Philharmonic with a baton – previously, the bow had normally been used. He then worked as the director of the Theater an der Wien, Vienna, then in 1820 was appointed director of the court theatre at Kassel. Although he occasionally quarelled with the Elector, his patron, he remained there for the rest of his life, valuing its security. Among his best-known works are the opera *Jessonda (1823),* his *Eighth Violin Concerto* and his *Nonet,* a very Schubertian piece.

Carl Maria Weber (1786-1826)

Born near Lubeck, Germany, Weber spent his early years travelling around with his father, who directed a theatrical company, getting to know the repertory of *Singspiel* (musical plays). Musically precocious, he championed German music – especially Mozart's *Singspiele* – against Italian fashions. This caused difficulties with the various posts he held (he resigned from the directorship of the Breslau opera house in protest at his reforms being spurned), but from 1817 he was director of the German repertory at the Dresden opera. In 1821 his most famous work, the romantic Singspiel *Der Freischuetz,* opened the new Berlin theatre and has kept Weber's name famous ever since. He died of tuberculosis in London in 1826, where he was conducting his opera *Oberon.* Weber was buried in London, but was later disinterred and reburied in Dresden; in tribute to the composer, Wagner gave an oration over the grave.

Bibliography

D. Arnold and N. Fortune (eds), *The Beethoven Companion,* Norton Press, New York, 1971

E. Blom, *Beethoven's Pianoforte Sonatas Discussed,* Da Capo Press, New York, 1968

V. D'Indy, *Beethoven: A Critical Biography,* Da Capo Press, New York, 1970

R. Fiske, *Beethoven Concertos and Overtures,* University of Washington Press, Seattle, 1970

R. James, *Beethoven* (Evergreen Lives), St. Martins Press, New York, 1972

A. Kalischer, *Beethoven's Letters,* Dover, New York, 1972

F. Knight, *Beethoven and the Age of Revolution,* International Publishing Corporation, New York, 1974

B. Lam, *Beethoven's String Quartets* (2 vols), University of Washington Press, Seattle, 1975

D. Matthews, *Beethoven Piano Sonatas,* University of Washington Press, Seattle, 1967

L. Misk, *Beethoven Studies,* University of Oklahoma Press, Norman, 1953

P. Nettl, *Beethoven Handbook,* Greenwood Press, New York, 1976

R. Simpson, *Beethoven Symphonies,* University of Washington Press, Seattle, 1971

M. Solomon, *Beethoven,* Schirner Books, New York, 1977

O. Sonneck, *Beethoven: Impressions by his Contemporaries,* Dover, New York, 1967

E. and R. Sterba, *Beethoven and His Nephew,* Pantheon Press, New York, 1954

J. Sullivan, *Beethoven: His Spiritual Development,* George Allen and Unwin, London, 1964

Listener's guide

This section examines in detail some of Beethoven's greatest and best-known works: the Pathétique, Moonlight and Appassionata piano sonatas, the 'Emperor' Concerto, the Violin Concerto in D and the Fifth Symphony. Together with sections on great interpreters of Beethoven's music and specific aspects of music development of relevance to the works under discussion (for example, the development of the piano and the evolution of the symphony), the descriptions of the pieces of music can be read independently as an examination of Beethoven's musical achievements. However, for the fullest appreciation of this great composer's music, the programme notes are better read before going to a live performance or while listening to the recorded music. The short accounts of the lives and works of some of Beethoven's contemporaries (see opposite) together with the Bibliography and the recommendations for further listening (within the text), suggest further areas of study should you wish to learn more about Beethoven's life, times and music.

Three piano sonatas

Beethoven's piano sonatas give us an immediate insight into his creative world. Works of vision and profound originality, they reflect Beethoven's own formidable powers as a pianist.

Although Beethoven's contribution to chamber music, the symphony and the concerto is immeasurable and a major influence in shaping 19th-century musical Romanticism, it is with the 32 piano sonatas that he gives us most ready access to his workshop, the nerve centre of his creative process. This is not to suggest that the piano works are in any way 'lighter' than, for instance, the string quartets, but reflects the fact that since Beethoven was a pianist – and from contemporary accounts one of the most formidable virtuosos of his day – the piano provided him with an

immediate creative outlet. It seems that his playing was sometimes 'muddled' but always 'full of character and temperament' and vehement enough 'to put a piano out of action'. Moreover, Beethoven was famous for his powers of improvising at the keyboard, and this freedom of musical fantasy finds its way into the piano music at an earlier stage than in the rest of his output. His 32 sonatas can be viewed in many different ways: from the First Sonata to the Arietta of the 32nd, op. 111, the listener is the intimate witness to a spiritual journey lasting nearly 30 years.

Grande sonate pathétique in C minor, op. 13

The *Pathétique* (1799) was the earliest sonata to achieve widespread popularity, and it is easy to see why. How many works are there which can communicate their mood and identity through the sound of their opening chord? Beethoven was famous for containing the germ of the whole work in one small phrase – the opening four notes of the Fifth Symphony, for example, that pervade the entire work – but his ability to recognize the power and drama latent in one chord of C Minor shows the strength and natural judgement of his inner ear. The other element that heightens the *Pathétique's* sense of identity is the slow introduction, a common enough device in the classical period, but which here goes against the norm by being absorbed into the structure of the first movement proper.

Programme notes

The Introduction is marked *Grave* (serious), and we hear the grim opening phrase three times, as it grows in discordant urgency. A brief scale passage discharges this tension by introducing a big, passionate melody which gives all the signs that the Introduction is going to develop into a complete movement.

Example 1

In the Pathétique *Sonata, Beethoven exploits the many moods of the piano. The beautiful, song-like second movement finds him exploring its more intimate qualities. Long phrases floated over a gentle accompaniment conjure up the lyrical world of Francis Danby's painting (left). Here, a lone figure muses by the sea against a backdrop of the setting sun.*

But this melody is quickly distorted and infected by recalls to the mood of the opening; the tension builds up again, and is skilfully diffused by a rapidly descending chromatic scale (in which every note, black as well as white, is played) that heralds the beginning of the fast movement – *Molto allegro e con brio* (very fast and with verve).

Over a rapid 'drum-roll' bass, the first subject erupts as though escaping from great tension. Because of the sharp contrast of the later repeats of the Introduction, the second subject, which

Mauro Pucciarelli

travels rapidly between bass and treble, sustains the mood of nervous intensity. This is reinforced at the end of the exposition by recalling the first subject in the key of the second. The rock-like solidity of the Introduction returns before the development darts away, playing with fragments of the link passage between first and second

During his early years in Vienna, Beethoven (above) became something of a celebrity – due in part to the generous patronage of the nobility. He dedicated the Pathétique Sonata *(1799) to Prince Lichnowsky, whose name appears on the title page (left).*

Beethoven-Haus, Bonn

subjects and the Introduction's passionate melody, the latter mockingly deflated. A long sustained bass note anticipates the return to the home key, which we hear with more of a sense of inevitability than release. A return to the Introduction momentarily breaks the flow before the terse, unyielding close.

What is remarkable about this movement is the relentless pace of the Allegro, with so little contrast of mood between the first and second groups. In a more conventional sonata layout, the contrasting second subject might have been the passionate melody from the Introduction, which, as we have seen, is only admitted in the development, cruelly distorted. To use change of tempo alone as the main means of contrast (one of the essential ingredients of sonata form) was a considerable and successful structural adventure.

The slow movement shows how dearly Beethoven valued the piano's gentler qualities. It is marked *Adagio cantabile* (slow and song-like), and the long phrases of the beautiful, hymn-like melody float effortlessly over a lightly scored accompaniment. The form of this movement is ternary, that is, a middle section flanked either side by similar material (ABA), but with modifications. The opening melody is interrupted by a short section with a slightly more agitated tune over a gently pulsating accompaniment. The contrasting

The title of the Moonlight *Sonata was coined by a German poet and musician, for whom the music evoked the haunting image of the moon shining on the still waters of a lake (right).*

Joseph Wright of Derby 'Matlock Tor by Moonlight'. Yale Center for British Art

Understanding music: the 'new testament' of the piano

Österreidrische Nationalbibliothek

The 32 sonatas of Beethoven played a crucial role in leading music away from the poise and elegance of the Classical style into the headier world of Romanticism.

Beethoven's piano sonatas are a unique document of the development of a musician's mind. They cover virtually the whole of his creative career: from the dashing exploits of a young lion at the keyboard, through the defiant heroism of his middle years, to the sublime mysteries he perceived at the end of his life. In contrast to the 'old testament' of keyboard music – Bach's *The Well-tempered Clavier,* consisting of 48 preludes and fugues – Beethoven's piano sonatas had a revolutionary effect upon instrumental style. They moved the piano away from the drawing-room elegance of Mozart's time and prepared it for the passionate pyrotechnics of the 19th century virtuosos such as Liszt and Thalberg.

In his boyhood Beethoven had first come to the attention of the public by performing fugues from Bach's '48'. The pianos of the time bore little resemblance to the concert grands of today. Small and lightly built, with a clear and silvery though weak tone, they were more akin to the harpsichord than the modern piano. In fact Beethoven's early sonatas are specified

45

middle section is in the minor key with a troubled figure in triplets (three equal notes played in the time normally occupied by two) that is worked into the texture at the return to the opening material.

The Finale is a rondo, where the opening theme (*ritornello* – the Italian word means 'little return') is played against contrasting 'episodes'. The form is here given added tautness by being cast as a sonata rondo: the deceptively innocent rondo theme

Example 2

is heard first, contrasted with a second

group of three themes in a different key. Beethoven's contemporaries tell us that the composer played this theme 'humorously'. The rondo theme is heard again before the appearance of new material – an episode with interweaving melodies that takes the place of a development. A dramatic descending scale announces the recapitulation, with rondo theme and second group all in C minor and major. There is a danger that the major key will upset the balance of mood, so Beethoven is careful to reassert strongly the minor key in the coda.

The key of C minor had a special signifi-

The autograph score of the Moonlight Sonata's *finale (below),* *with Beethoven's* *rapid and agitated markings.*

Malvisi Archives

Beethoven dedicated the Moonlight Sonata **to the 17-year-old Countess Guilietta Guicciardi (above) – 'a dear charming girl . . . whom I love'.**

Beethoven-Haus, Bonn/Giraudon

as being suitable for either instrument, though to be fair to their composer, this was in all probability a publisher's trick to try and catch as large a sale as possible. For this was the age of transition, when the harpsichord was not quite dead and the new-fangled piano not yet in every home. It took most of the 18th century for the piano to assume its position of superiority over the harpsichord, and Haydn, Mozart and Beethoven grew up with both.

Beethoven's first sonatas were dedicated to his teacher Haydn, whose music they resemble much more closely than that of the younger Mozart. There is a gruffness and edge about them that is largely lacking in Mozart's eloquent and exquisitely turned pieces for the instrument. They rely much more on dramatic contrast and discussion of themes than upon the elegant statement of long-spanned melody. In his early years the sonatas were – for Beethoven – relatively conventional, using the typical five-octave compass of the time and making technical demands that most competent amateur pianists can cope with. However, the thin and relatively feeble sound of the

early pianos was far from adequate to meet Beethoven's growing pianistic needs, and as his composer friend Anton Reicha reported:

He asked me to turn the pages, but I was too busy wrenching the strings out of the piano as they broke, while the hammers got jammed among them. But Beethoven insisted on finishing the piece, so I hopped to and fro pulling the strings, freeing the hammers and turning the pages. I worked harder than Beethoven.

Thus by 1803, when he had acquired an Erard grand piano, Beethoven was able to exploit its greater potential to the utmost in the massive *Waldstein* Sonata op. 53. In Beethoven's last sonatas, from op. 101 onwards, the demands made on the pianist become even more immense: the mighty *Hammerklavier* Sonata op. 106 and the variations that form the Finale of his last sonata op. 111 require a technique of consummate virtuosity. This is not to say that the music got progressively bigger and better as its composer developed: there

are movements of monumental power in the early sonatas and miniatures of exquisite form and loveliness in the later works. But it is largely a pointless, though pleasurable, task to extol the merits of any particular movement or work against another. There is scarcely a weak moment anywhere in the entire canon of the 32 sonatas. Beethoven was not a rapid composer, and the creation of music did not come easily to him. Accordingly each of these pieces is a result of the most careful thought and construction, with the rejection of many initial drafts in favour of the final and most satisfying result. However spontaneous the music may sound, it is composed with the most meticulous and intellectual craftsmanship that is unmatched in the piano works of any other composer.

With his 'new testament' of the piano, Beethoven took the form as he inherited it from Haydn and Mozart and stretched it to breaking point, but in the process he invested it with such flexibility and dramatic power that it still sounds startlingly original today.

cance for Beethoven and he frequently turned to it for his larger works in a minor key, for example in the Third Piano Concerto and the Fifth Symphony. It is well suited to the *Pathétique* (the full title of the Sonata is Beethoven's own) as it conveys a mood of tragedy and pathos. And even though the gravitational pull is towards the elaborate first movement, all three movements complement each other in their sequence of mood.

Sonata in C sharp minor, op. 27 no. 2 ('Moonlight')

Beethoven's meteoric rise to fame during his early years in Vienna was due largely to the liberal patronage he received from the nobility. Music was central to the city's glittering social life, and Beethoven's talent and eccentricity ensured that he was much in demand at the grandest salons. In this he was no doubt helped by his teacher Haydn and his benefactor in Bonn, Count Wald-stein, who also provided him with letters of introduction. So, very soon after his arrival in Vienna, Beethoven was able to take lodgings in the house of Prince Karl Lichnowsky, who became his foremost patron.

His bold and original piano playing astounded the Viennese audiences and his compositions soon aroused as much interest. It is not difficult to imagine the anticipation that would attend the first performance of a new sonata; moreover, the person to whom the work was dedi-cated was guaranteed some measure of posterity when the work was printed by the ever growing number of publishers eager to add Beethoven to their lists. Prince Lichnowsky, for example, was the dedicatee of the *Pathétique,* and the Countess Giulietta Guicciardi that of the *Moonlight* Sonata.

The *Moonlight* was written in 1801, the year in which Beethoven admitted in letters to his growing fears about his deafness, and it is in one of these letters that he also writes: 'I am now leading a slightly more pleasant life, for I am mixing more with my fellow creatures . . . This change has been brought about by a dear, charming girl, who loves me and whom I love . . . Unfortunately, she is not of my class, and at the moment I certainly could not marry.' The 'dear, charming girl' was the 17-year-old Countess, one of Beethoven's piano pupils, who may also have been the inspiration for the slow movement of the String Quartet op. 18 no. 1, intended as a tone painting of the tomb scene from Romeo and Juliet.

Programme notes

The Sonata's nickname was coined by a German poet and musician, Ludwig Rellstab, who likened the first movement to the moonlight shining on the water of Lake Lucerne. It is certainly one of

P. J. de Loutherbourg 'The Shipwreck' Château-Musée de Dieppe/Bulloz

Beethoven's most original conceptions, and its dreamy, improvisatory quality explores the sonorities of the piano in a way that anticipates the impressionist world of Debussy by nearly a hundred years. It is based on the simplest material. A seamless flow of triplets undulates in the middle of the texture; these still waters are given depth by an implacable, measured bass, and over the surface there sounds an eerie fragment of melody, like the mournful call of a horn. Woven into this call is a dotted (long/short) figure, which is just enough to propel the music with a sense of gentle ebb and flow.

The middle of the movement is tonally restless before returning to the opening material, and in the short coda the melody (such as it is) is silenced as the long/short rhythm slips quietly into the bass. There is a hint of menace in this movement, and its remoteness is emphasized by the instructions to the player to play as quietly as possible, with the damper pedal pressed down (except at the change of harmony) to allow the strings to vibrate freely.

This mysterious, darkly coloured mood is alleviated by the middle movement, an elegant Allegretto, whose fragile poise is shaken by the syncopations (displaced rhythm) of the middle Trio section.

The suggestion of hidden menace in the first movement uncoils violently in the Finale, a fully realized sonata movement and one of the most vivid storm movements Beethoven had yet written. It is marked *Presto agitato* (very fast and agitated), and the first subject is hardly a theme, but rather a rapid succession of ascending arpeggios punctuated by two violent chords. Out of this turbulence there emerges the second subject, different by being a new melody in a new key,

Example 3

but still part of the same violent mood of the opening. The exposition continues with a third subject, a repeated chord figure that grows in strength, only to be wound down in the short codetta.

The development is based mainly on fragments of the opening of the second subject which falls menacingly into the bass under a persistent *tremolando* ('trembling') in the right hand (an effect produced by a rapid alternation of two notes). It comes to a brief moment of repose in two solemn

The turbulent, storm-tossed mood of the Appassionata *suggests a scene of shipwreck (left). Beethoven's pupil Carl Czerny described it as a stormy sea on a dark night and a distant cry for help.*

chords before the recapitulation recalls the turmoil of the opening.

Music of such red hot energy is going to need a closing section of great strength to put the brakes on and bring about a satisfactory close; even by Beethoven's standards, the coda of the *Moonlight* is both arresting and effective. A series of hurried spread chords gives way to a recall of the second subject, first in the bass (as in the development), then bursting upwards, gathering momentum in a string of arpeggios which culminate in a trill with a short cadenza. This peters out into another moment of repose, recalling the moment of recapitulation, before the tempo picks up and moves the music to a tense, dramatic close.

Beethoven called both Sonatas of the op.

Beethoven composed the **Appassionata** *at the castle home of Prince Lichnowsky. However, following a heated exchange, he stormed out into the pouring rain. This may account for the rain-spattered manuscript (right).*

The powerful drama and tragedy of the **Appassionata** *are reflected in Rubens's vigorous drawing (below).*

27 set Sonatas *quasi una fantasia* (like a fantasy) and instructed that the movements of the *Moonlight* should follow each other without a break. The way the work gradually opens out into the complexity of the finale provides a gathering sense of climax, hinted at in the veiled power of the first movement. Beethoven's sonatas at this time were full of experiments, as he sought to reassess the underlying principles of sonata form. In general, sonatas often only followed the conventional layout of sonata form in one movement, usually the first. But it did not take Beethoven long to break the mould. The *Moonlight* was one of the works that started the move from Classical to Romantic music.

Sonata in F minor, op. 57 (Appassionata)

Only three years separate the *Moonlight* from the *Appassionata* Sonata (the title was added by the publisher), written in 1804–5. During that time there were two significant events in Beethoven's life. The first was his writing of the so-called Heiligenstadt Testament of 1802, the despairing document in which Beethoven acknowledged the likelihood of permanent deafness and, although he would not commit suicide, declared himself ready for death. The second, in sharp contrast to this low point of despondency, was the composition of the *Eroica* Symphony, a work which, like Wagner's *Tristan und Isolde,* is a touchstone in the development of European music. In both works the poise of Classical form is revitalized to cope with the more extreme demands of Romantic expression.

The strength and size of the *Appassionata's* four movements and the lofty idealism of its musical content are displayed on the grandest canvas. The sheer weight of symphonic thought and the listener's feeling that he is witness to a personal narrative also ennoble the sonata, giving it a scope and drama that Beethoven had not achieved in earlier works.

Programme notes

The first movement opens with a cavernous theme that picks out the notes of the F minor chord, but repeated a semitone higher. Soon we hear a sinister four-note figure (anticipating the fate motif right at the start of the Fifth Symphony) that winds up the tension to what appears to be a return to the opening, but is transformed by sequences of massive, upward moving, crashing chords. A link passage over a repeated-note bass introduces the second subject in A flat, the relative major.

Example 4

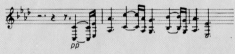

Whereas the first subject travelled down then up, so this melody moves first up then down, but is obviously closely related by sharing the same rhythm. The mood darkens as the music changes to A flat minor, and a long winding solo scale passage reintroduces the turbulent mood of the opening, with an ominous figure in the bass stalking abruptly

upwards. Soon, however, the music runs out of steam, the exposition coming to a temporary close on two A flats five octaves apart (at the top and the bottom of the keyboard).

The development takes a fragment of the opening subject, throwing it wildly from hand to hand. The second subject reappears, this time more unstable, and breaks loose from its previous lyricism in a series of violent spread chords. The sinister four-note figure (noticeably absent so far in the development) heralds the recapitulation, but goes on sounding, levelling out into repeated notes as the first subject steals in. The effect is unsettling, because it still feels as though the development is going on. These repeated notes do not relax their grip until the crashing chords reappear, this time in triumphant F major, handing on a statement of the second subject still in the major.

But the troubled minor has its say as the turbulent mood again gathers force to a coda that starts in the same way as the development, expands hugely in an anguished succession of arpeggios that resound over the entire keyboard, and

fizzles out in a recall of the four-note figure, pathetic and exposed as it slumps to a temporary Adagio. It abruptly pulls itself together to announce *fortissimo* the closing passage, where the main theme emerges, swinging back and forth. A few bars of aggressively rhythmic chords yield to the main theme which subsides quietly and quickly to a close, but in such a way that, although the movement is over, there is still the feeling that there is much more to come.

The Andante is a theme with four variations. The solemn *chorale* (hymn-like) theme is heard in the tenor and bass register of the piano, moving upwards as the first three variations acquire more and more decoration; the fourth variation returns to the solemnity of the opening. Two mysterious chords, one soft, the second loud, lead into a jarring fanfare that heralds the finale. The tragic, storm-tossed mood returns in a whirling *moto perpetuo* ('perpetually moving' passage), which repeats the development and recapitulation in order to give more tension to the dramatic *Presto* (very fast) section that brings the sonata to a breathless conclusion.

Great interpreters

Wilhelm Kempff (pianist)

When the time comes to single out this century's truly great interpreters of Beethoven at the keyboard, along with such legends as Schnabel, Solomon and Gieseking will be the name of Wilhelm Kempff. And although his name took longer than the others to become internationally established, his reputation is now impregnable.

Kempff was born in 1895 in the Prussian town of Jüterbog, close to Berlin. His was a musical family that had close ties with the church – both his father and grandfather were organists there. In fact, his earliest musical training was under his father. At the age of nine he was admitted to the Berlin Hochschule für Musik, studying both piano and composition. Through his teacher there, Heinrich Barth, he could claim direct links with Beethoven, as Barth had been a pupil of Liszt, and Liszt a pupil of Carl Czerny, who was himself a pupil of Beethoven's. This influence is perhaps discernible in his ability to improvise brilliantly at a moment's notice, which very few classical performers can do. His studies in music were rounded off at University, where he also took courses in philosophy and the history of music.

By 1918 Kempff had made his début with the Berlin Philharmonic under Nikisch, and in the following years he undertook tours in Europe, followed by concerts in South America and Japan. This pattern, plus his commitment to teaching new talents, was kept up until the outbreak of World War II. During the 1930s he gave summer classes, along with Edwin Fischer

Deutsche Grammophon Produktion

and Walter Gieseking, at Potsdam.

Since the war, Kempff has both continued his teaching commitments – if anything, intensifying them as the years passed – and broadened his performing career, making his début in England in 1951, and his US début at the surprisingly late date of 1964. His recording career has been long and distinguished and his position in the music world today is that of a revered master. He is also the author of a vivid autobiography and a composer in his own right.

Piano Concerto no. 5 in E flat, op. 73

Beethoven's last piano concerto was also his greatest. Known as the 'Emperor' in English, the nickname endures as a tribute to the work's lasting stature as an emperor among concertos.

Beethoven completed his Fifth Piano Concerto in 1809, the year in which Napoleon and his all-conquering *Grande Armée* attacked and took Vienna. In the cellar of a friend's house the composer tied pillows over his head, not because he was a coward, but because he wanted to save what little was left of his hearing. Elsewhere in Vienna, Beethoven's great predecessor and teacher, the composer Haydn, lay dying. He was 77, and he passed away in May, not long after the city had capitulated.

The Viennese, whose imperial family had departed a week before the bombardment, were no match for Napoleon, but at least this time they tried to defend their city. Back in 1805, they had simply given in to Napoleon's Marshal Murat. Yet the populace was so short of arms that lances, guns and sabres were taken from the property rooms of the state theatres to be used by the troops. They were of little use. After just over a week, the city fell.

Beethoven was, understandably, distraught during the experience. Later he wrote to his publishers, Breitkopf and Härtel, about this period and of how the events had affected him, body and soul. He told of his frustration at not being able to get out into his beloved countryside, while all around him there was nothing but the sound of drums, guns and armed men, as well as every sort of war-time misery.

The 'Emperor'?

The 'Emperor' Concerto was not so named after Napoleon; in fact this nickname did not derive from Beethoven. The composer had indeed been an admirer of General Bonaparte when he had seemed destined to release Europe from tyranny, but it was precisely Napoleon's elevation as an emperor, and his career as a conqueror, that alienated the composer's esteem. So how did the Concerto get its name? In fact, it is only used in English-speaking countries, and it was probably coined by the piano-making composer and music publisher, J. B. Cramer, a German who settled in Britain. Probably, he simply said that the work was an emperor among concertos.

Few would deny this claim, assuming Cramer made it. The Concerto is magnificent, its first movement splendid and triumphant, the slow movement spell-bindingly beautiful, the finale, exuberant, exultant and nobly expansive. But Donald Tovey, the revered scholar, composer and pianist, thought that the Concerto's acquired title was vulgar. 'So we will say no more about it,' he sniffed, 'but attend to the music.' Today, however, most music-lovers are happy with the Concerto's popular title, for, in the widest, grandest sense of the word, it does indeed rank gloriously high.

The first performance

Though the 'Emperor' was finished in 1809, it was not given its first performance until two years later, on 28 November, 1811. Considering Beethoven's fame by this time, the long delay must surely have been due to the troubled times in which it was completed. Beethoven dedicated his new Concerto to Archduke Rudolph of Austria, his pupil, patron and friend. The Archduke was a friend in deed as well as word. Before leaving Vienna when the French were approaching, he guaranteed an income (along with two other admirers of the composer) to ensure that Beethoven remained in Vienna.

Beethoven was now too deaf to give the Concerto its first performance. Because of this, he wrote the solo part out in full, which he had not done in the past because he had been his own soloist at his premières. The pianist entrusted with the all-important first performance was Friedrich Schneider, and the orchestra was the very fine Gewandhaus Orchestra of Leipzig, conducted by Johann Schultz. Happily, the performance was a triumph for Beethoven. According to the influential newspaper, *Allgemeine Musikalische Zeitung,* the first audience was so enthusiastic that it could scarcely content itself with ordinary signs of recognition and enjoyment. Alas, three months later, on 12 February 1812, the Viennese première was far less successful. The soloist was Carl Czerny, one of Beethoven's pupils, who is best remembered now as the composer of instructive works for the piano but was then a notable composer and teacher, as well as a fine pianist. But the Concerto was received with far less enthusiasm than at Leipzig. One critic wrote that Beethoven was too proud and over confident, and that he had written 'above' his audience. This comment probably reflects the relative conservatism of Viennese audiences, who

were less open than the citizens of Leipzig had been to innovative music.

The process of composition

Beethoven was prepared to work and work on his Fifth Piano Concerto until he had satisfied his most demanding critic — himself. His sketchbooks show that the magical beauty of the slow movement did not come at all easily. Perfection may have flowed from Mozart, but Beethoven had to strive mightily and continually to achieve it, for his was a genius of a different kind.

Historisches Museum der Stadt Wien

Even comparative newcomers to Beethoven's music soon begin to be aware of the way his musical life developed in power, passion and depth. So while the Fifth Concerto can be enjoyed by a newcomer to music in splendid isolation from what had gone before, it can be appreciated also as the finest concerto of Beethoven's career.

His early concertos followed the conventions that had been brought to perfection by Mozart. But, instead of the usual long orchestral introduction followed by the appearance of the soloist, Beethoven's Fourth opens with a few most beautiful bars of piano music. Again, in his Violin Concerto of 1806, four drum beats open the Concerto, followed by a quiet woodwind melody. They form an unconventionally quiet but gripping opening to a masterpiece.

The 'Emperor' required slightly bigger forces than had the Fourth, which is scored for flute, two oboes, two clarinets, two bassoons, two horns, two trumpets, kettledrums and strings. The 'Emperor' lists slightly more, with two flutes, four horns, but is otherwise the same. It inhabits the heroic world of the *Eroica* and Fifth Symphonies, but it is the grand climax of Beethoven's commitment to the development of the piano as the major instrument for the expression of passion and feeling. The 'Emperor' was destined to be Beethoven's last piano concerto, though he began on another one which was never completed.

As mortars drop bombs on the old city, Napoleon's troops prepare to occupy Vienna (above). While the siege raged in 1809, Beethoven wrote his last piano concerto – the Fifth. Its English nickname arose from its stature as a great concerto – an 'Emperor' among concertos, as bold and defiant as Napoleon (left) himself.

Programme notes

However it originated, the Concerto's English nickname endured because it seemed to express the power and majesty of the music. And, when considering the music, it is worth following the emperor idea to see what light it sheds. Certainly, there is a distinctly regal quality about the first movement, and perhaps it is not too fanciful to see the role of the piano in its dialogue with the orchestra as that of an emperor with his empire, represented by his court, cabinet, or subjects – in line with the true nature of the classical concerto as an argument between the individual and society.

First movement – Allegro

The work opens with a ceremonial chord asserting the key of E flat major. The piano enters with a cadenza-like passage usually reserved for the close of a movement;

At the Concerto's first performance Friedrich Schneider (above right) was the soloist, although Beethoven had hoped to be able to play the piano himself. In 1811 it was published (above), but the publishers, Breitkopf & Härtel, were so careless that they earned Beethoven's rebuke: 'Mistakes, mistakes! You are a great mistake yourself!'

The spirited, exhilarating clamour of the first movement suggest the energy of a royal hunt. Prancing steeds, echoing horns and baying dogs all move in an intense and eager anticipation of triumph.

obviously the rather unusual royal personage represented here by the soloist is not too bothered about court protocol. This bravura passage explores the implications of that opening chord, and of subsequent chords interjected by the orchestra, using the very simplest musical elements – scales, arpeggios, trills – almost in the manner of an improvisation: these are the laws of the musical empire from our imaginary emperor's point of view. But the emperor is not that decisive a ruler – although at times he can be quite imperious – and seems in danger of getting carried away by over-elaboration. Eventually he returns to the point with three quiet chords. He has had the opening say; the court can now get down to affairs of state. Throughout the work these roles will be maintained, although at times the monarch seems to conform more to the traditional idea of a feminine ruler contrasting with a masculine court – a queen or empress

perhaps? – softening the harsh reality of the orchestral statements, interceding to ask for more time, or for a more merciful treatment of a subject before resuming the command of the orchestra as the imperial majesty.

The orchestra now gets down to business with the first theme, a rather bustling march that brooks no delay.

Example 1

At this point it is worth noting the tremendous tension and momentum that Beethoven sets and maintains until the end of the movement. This is the very energy of good government, in which Beethoven was such an ardent believer.

A great procession of themes parades past in this masterly opening, which loses

no time in moving regularly from one to another, amid rhythmic drum beats and descending brass. Most conspicuous is the second subject.

Example 2

It appears in three versions. First, as a *staccato pianissimo* (abrupt but very soft) in the minor for the strings, then as a soft duet for mellow horns over drums, and finally, as a triumphal march for full orchestra.

By using this theme in different versions and playing them simultaneously, Beethoven gives a new twist to them, and uses this technique to throw the listener off balance. The two versions are even played out of phase, giving great subtlety and a kind of syncopation to basically very

Understanding music: themes and variations

Traditionally the composer's main problem has been to write an extended piece of music that will still have a recognizable shape for the listener. The answer was to subject a tune to a series of variations. In the 16th and 17th centuries, before a workable system of useful major and minor keys, and key relationships, had been established, sets of variations were far and away the most common examples of extended instrumental composition. The theme would often be a popular song which would generally be subjected to decoration of ever-increasing complexity, while the bass-line, or inner parts, would also become progressively more florid as the piece went on. John Bull's *The King's Hunt,* where the Elizabethan composer used his virtuosity to suggest jingling harnesses, ringing hoofbeats, hunting-horns and the leaping of hedges, is a delightful example.

Variations continued to be popular in the 18th century even though a system of key-changing through the use of major and minor scales enabled composers to extend their music by other means. The mightiest keyboard work to come out of the 18th century is J. S. Bach's *Goldberg* Variations. The theme is a slow, highly-ornamented *sarabande* (dance tune) that is subjected to 30 variations.

The first Classical masters, Haydn and Mozart, also enjoyed the variation form; and being above all composers of melody, they used melodic variation. Haydn was fond of using a set of variations as a slow movement in his symphonies: the blithe little theme in the slow movement of his *Surprise* symphony (no. 94 in G) must be the most famous example. In his concertos, chamber and instrumental music Mozart liked to insert a slow variation in his generally cheerful music – as if he wanted to look at the tune he used from all angles before putting it aside.

Of the many variations that Beethoven wrote the greatest were the *Diabelli* Piano Variations. Anton Diabelli was a successful music publisher and hack composer, who had the idea of asking 50 composers (among them Schubert and the infant Liszt) each to write a variation on a silly waltz-theme he had made up. As if to show the world what he could wrest from such unpromising material, Beethoven responded not with one variation but with 33. Schubert had a unique gift for melody and, by extension, for melodic variation. He used his own melodies as themes, sometimes drawn from songs he had written, such as the life-enhancing little set in the *Trout* Quintet.

A contemporary of Schubert, the great violin virtuoso Paganini, wrote a little set of variations on an original theme in one of the violin Caprices that has since become world famous. Brahms, Rachmaninov, Boris Blacher and even Andrew Lloyd Weber have found it an ideal vehicle for all kinds of variation: melodic, harmonic and simply rhythmical. Brahms, something of a musical antiquarian, wrote Romantic sets of variations in a rather severe classical mould: the lovely *St Antony* Variations for orchestra, and a set for piano on a theme of Handel are his two masterpieces in variation form.

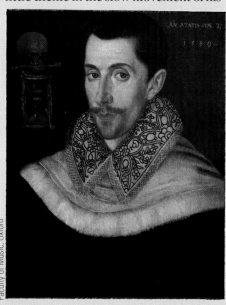

The Elizabethan composer John Bull and a page from his The King's Hunt.

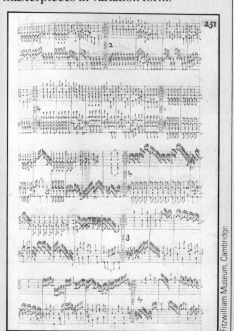

The hauntingly lovely face of Botticelli's Venus seems to hold a hint of sadness. The expression captures the exquisite tenderness of the Concerto's second movement, which is soon dispersed by a more vigorous conclusion.

simple melodies. The first time this rocking theme is heard, the melody is shared in a cross rhythm between *pizzicato* (plucked) strings and *legato* (smooth and flowing) bassoon and clarinet; the second time it is shared between horns and drums; and the third time, after a passage where the strings wind themselves up, it is blared out by the full orchestra. The majestic exposition ends with some thumping chords, and the piano enters again with a quiet chromatic scale to begin the consideration and development of all the great themes that have been put to it. At first it is quite content to provide a mere accompaniment while the orchestra discusses the first theme; but gradually the rhythm gets more insistent and leads to a great stormy climax, with the piano going into a rage of octaves, contradicting its colleagues by ascending while the orchestra is descending, and vice versa. The harmonies become more and more discordant, but the storm abates and concord returns.

The orchestra takes advantage of this relaxation to bring in a hint of the first theme, with a sinister version of the first phrase repeated insistently to bring about a recapitulation of the opening, with the piano repeating its entry. The piano provides some even lovelier adornment before a chord, or bargain, is struck for a cadenza. Here Beethoven has written specific instructions for the soloist: 'Do not play a cadenza, but attack immediately the following.' He doesn't want to lose the effect of compression at this point, and keeps the cadenza to a further exploration of the two main themes. Then the horns calmly lead the movement's close.

Second movement – Adagio un poco mosso
The slow movement begins softly with a hymn-like tune on violins and violas (the violins muted) to a pizzicato accompaniment on the double basses.

Example 3

As the celestial melody progresses, clarinets and bassoons add a touch of colour before the soloist is ushered in with great solemnity.

However, the piano seems at first almost to ignore the orchestra's lead with this beautiful theme. Its delicate adornments seem a distracted improvisation on the pursuit of its own line of thought, although there are teasing references to the second half of the melody. The strings, somewhat awed by the beauty of this reflective waywardness, respectfully remind the piano of the opening theme, repeating the upward climbing closing phrases, which only bring some more beautiful prevarication from the soloist in a sequence of descending chromatic scales. Now it is the turn of the oboes and horns to say 'Hey, what about our tune?' But the piano will have nothing to do with it, and distances itself from the orchestra, turning inwards as if saying — 'Just leave me be, and I'll show you what I've got for you.'

Expectancy rises, but the piano keeps the orchestra on the edge of its seat, making it guess what is to follow. This is a most marvellous dialogue. The trills are punctuated by single notes from the strings saying 'Yes' and 'What?' The trills rise higher and higher, and then spill over to show what the piano had been keeping up its sleeve all along — a most beautiful *cantabile* (singing) version of the first theme (Example 3). There is a grateful pizzicato from the strings, as if to say 'Now at last you're talking sense,' and the piano gracefully replies, 'Well, it's your turn now. I'll accompany you. See what you can come up with.'

The orchestra does in fact come up with a new variation on woodwind led by the flute, which the piano accompanies in a somewhat devious manner, using a sequence of notes that contain the melody, but always played a split second later than the orchestra. In fact, the piano is still determined to have its own way, and is planning sabotage as its accompaniment leads the perplexed orchestra into a strange no man's land of repetitive phrases. Finally, the orchestra falls silent save for a sustained B on the bassoons, the original key note of the movement. Then horns play a semitone lower, giving us a prophetic B flat, which transforms the whole scene.

Then the piano quietly comes up with the idea it has been hatching for some time — the theme of the following finale tentatively played in the tempo of this dying slow movement.

Third movement – Allegro ma non troppo

The theme turns out to be a jolly peasant dance and at the start of the movement the piano is ready to jump into the arena with it — a cartwheeling, tumbler-like tune, merry with trills. The differences between orchestra and soloist — emperor and court — are now over and the orchestra joins in the celebrations.

Now there is equal opportunity for virtuosity rather than a conflict of ideas, and the tunes throughout the movement are tossed from one section to another, for all to share. The brass section sound a rhythmic figure which will return again to bind the movement together, showing Beethoven's masterly grip on the proceedings.

Rhythmic punctuations of this figure send the piano scampering to find another, more lyrical tune, ending with laughing comments from the bassoon and then the clarinet, which the piano imitates. The repeated rhythmic figure on strings leads to a sadder version of the tune in another key – A flat – and then in an even remoter key – E major.

Then a marvellous passage follows, where under prolonged trills on the piano, the violins with broken phrases remind us of how the whole thing started at the end of the slow movement.

Finally, the drum accompanies the slowing down of the movement, coming through the piano part to reveal the bare bones. But it is the stalwart piano's job to provide the final volcanic flourish.

Joseph Wright's image of Vesuvius erupting complements the closing moment when, the piano returns to finish the Concerto in a blazing outburst.

Joseph Wright of Derby 'Eruption of Vesuvius'. Derby Art Gallery

Bernard Haitink (above) and the Concertgebouw Orchestra (right).

Phonogram International

Great interpreters

Beethoven's Fifth Piano Concerto has attracted varied interpretations from a large number of conductors and pianists, but one of the greatest is that by the combination of the conductor Bernard Haitink, the pianist Claudio Arrau and the Concertgebouw Orchestra. Arrau reveals the fire and majesty of Beethoven's works in its two outer movements, while keeping a perfect tension and lyricism in the beautiful second movement, *adagio un poco mosso.* His depth of understanding of the work is equally matched by that of the conductor and orchestra in every detail. Concertgebouw enjoys a distinguished reputation throughout the world and its partnership with Haitink and Arrau makes their interpretation of the Fifth Piano Concerto one of power and sensitivity.

FURTHER LISTENING

Piano Concerto no. 4 in G, op. 58
This is the first piano concerto in which Beethoven made a decisive break in his methods from the more classically-framed preceding pieces. Using striking themes and rhythmic motifs, he weaves a fascinating musical odyssey, bringing both piano and orchestra in from the first bars – a rare practice at the time – and never deviating significantly throughout the Concerto from the poetic mood he has created. In this least aggressive of all his piano concertos, the flow of inspiration is nonetheless unstoppable.

Fidelio, op. 72
Beethoven wrote only one opera: unlike Mozart, who could turn his magic to good use on literally any theme or idea and bless even the most idiotic libretto with his music, Beethoven felt very strongly about what were morally fit subjects for opera and what were not. Accordingly, he found very few stories to his taste. *Fidelio,* then, has as its intertwining themes the triumph of love, purity, heroism and honour over evil. But moral purity is not its only merit. It also contains a good deal of Beethoven's most noble music, and is a model of formal and dramatic balance.

'Kreutzer' Sonata, op.47
Beethoven revolutionized the whole basis for violin-piano sonatas, raising the violin for the first time to the level of an equal partner in the musical debate. And the 'Kreutzer' Sonata of 1802 is perhaps the first masterpiece in this revised genre, exhibiting intense passion and a complete intellectual mastery in the musical interplay and its constant development of the basic themes. As such it is a crucial work. It is also very beautiful.

Violin Concerto in D, op. 61

Beethoven's Violin Concerto is often described as a work of perfection. Containing some of the most sublime passages ever written for the violin, it inhabits a world of beauty and tranquillity

Four quiet drum beats open Beethoven's Violin Concerto, and they are answered by a serene, flowing melody played by the orchestral woodwind. This lovely theme immediately establishes the mood of tranquillity which above all pervades the work. The originality of this opening is striking – there are no conventional flourishes or theatrical effects – and, it is worth noting in passing, that so far we have heard neither the solo violin nor the orchestral strings.

The general character of this great concerto is persuasive rather than declamatory. Compare it, for example, with Beethoven's Fifth Symphony, or with the Fifth ('Emperor') Piano Concerto – works of overwhelming power. There was, though, another more intimate side to Beethoven's art. The Fourth Piano Concerto, in G major, was completed just before the Violin Concerto was written (1806), and this too is predominantly a gentle work. This is not to suggest that these works lack drama or power: it is simply that the drama is not of the tub-thumping kind. The composer evidently saw no reason why a concerto with orchestra should not be both thoughtful and graceful, and indeed he spelt out his intentions in an inscription to the violinist who gave the work its première and for whom the Concerto was written, Franz Clement: 'Concerto par Clemenza pour Clement, primo Violino e Direttore al Theatro a Vienne dal L. v. Bthvn, 1806'. (Concerto by Clemency for Clement, leading violinist and director at the theatre in Vienna, from L. van Beethoven, 1806).

'Clemency', as well as meaning 'merci-fulness', denotes 'mildness of temper'. Perhaps that was a quality Beethoven did not always reveal to his friends – he could be impatient and rough – but it is certainly often to be found in his music. The Violin Concerto is full of tenderness, feeling and a kind of delicate warmth. Perhaps the inscription to Clement was an avowal of feelings that the composer could rarely express in his human relationships. Typically, however, he conceals it with a rather clumsy pun. But the Concerto itself speaks clearly enough: and where a work

like the Fifth Symphony above all embodies strength, here we seem to hear the voice of love.

Beethoven and the violin

'Beethoven was a pianist, not a violinist', declares George R. Marek in his biography of the composer, and yet 'he created the Mount Everest of violin concertos . . . encompassing grandeur and mystery,

The persuasive beauty of Beethoven's Violin Concerto is reflected in Savery's painting of 'Orpheus' (right). Seated in an idyllic landscape, playing a violin, Orpheus entices the animals out of the forests and inspires the birds to dip and soar on high.

Beethoven composed his Violin Concerto in 1806, when he was in his mid-30s (far left). It was written especially for the violinist Franz Clement (1780–1842), who, from the age of eight (centre left) had delighted the public with his graceful and sensitive violin playing. Beethoven heard him in 1794 and in 1806 attended Franz Clement's benefit concert for the première of his Violin Concerto. The programme (left) included several other works, and among them a 'circus-trick' composition of Clement's own. Clement played the Violin Concerto at sight – for Beethoven, as usual, had not completed the work until the last moment.

sweetness and humour'. However, elsewhere in his biography, Marek writes, seemingly paradoxically, the following: 'Organist, violinist, violist, cembalist [harpsichordist], he was all of these'.

Beethoven did indeed study the violin, as a boy, with the teacher Franz Ries. One of his fellow pupils was his friend Stephan von Breuning – and it can hardly be coincidence that 20 years later he dedicated the published score of the Violin Concerto to him. (The work was written for the violinist Clement, but dedicated to von Breuning.) The young Beethoven became proficient enough as a string player to play in the orchestra of the Bonn Court Theatre from about 1789 – admittedly as a viola player rather than a violinist, but the instruments are essentially similar in technique. It is true, however, that after he settled in Vienna in 1792 his success as a pianist and composer meant that he increasingly neglected the violin. There is a story dating from around 1798 of how Beethoven's violin playing was received by a violinist friend, Karl Amenda:

B. complained that he could not get along on the violin. Asked by A. to try it, nevertheless, he played so fearfully that A. had to call out, 'Have mercy – quit!' B. quit playing and the two laughed till they had to hold their sides.

But even if he came to neglect the violin as a player, Beethoven continued to compose for the instrument. In 1792 he had started, and then abandoned, a violin concerto, and the following years saw him writing string trios and string quartets, violin sonatas and two romances for violin and orchestra. The Violin Concerto in D major, op. 81 was written in 1806 and performed later in the same year.

The first performance
Franz Clement, the brilliant young violinist who gave Beethoven's Concerto its

As a boy, Beethoven took violin lessons from Franz Ries (above). It appears that he was almost painful to listen to, although he seems to have been tolerably proficient on the viola. His viola (left) is now kept in the Beethoven House in Bonn.

première, was born in Vienna in 1780 and died there in 1842. As a boy and young man he travelled a good deal as an instrumentalist before settling down from 1802–11 as the conductor at the Theater an der Wien. Beethoven knew him from about this time. Subsequently Clement was to travel again (Eastern Europe and Germany) before finally returning to his native city to die a poor man.

Violinist, composer and conductor, Clement was a versatile musician and, it seems, a thoughtful and sensitive one. According to one writer, 'his style as a violinist was not vigorous, nor was his tone very powerful: gracefulness and tenderness of expression were its main characteristics'. It would seem that in writing his Concerto especially for Clement, Beethoven was conscious of these qualities. He wrote the work very rapidly. According to his pupil Carl Czerny, he did it 'pretty well straight through', and it was only just prior to Clement's benefit concert that the orchestral parts were finished, so that there was literally no time for a proper rehearsal. As for the concert itself, on 23 December 1806, this was, to say the least, unfortunately laid out. For one thing, the new Concerto was split up, the first movement being played before and the other two after the interval. It was not only the interval which broke the musical continuity – the audience heard, among other things, a sonata of Clement's own composition, played on one string with the violin upside down.

It looks as if Clement must have thought Beethoven's Concerto too long and intellectual to present to the public without a break. Critical opinion, too, was cautious, as in the *Zeitung für Theater, Musik und Poesie* (8 January 1807):

A division of opinion exists about Beethoven's Concerto. Some acknowledge much beauty in it, while others feel that its continuity seems often broken and that an endless repetition of commonplace passages is fatiguing . . . One fears that if Beethoven pursues his

The title page to the published edition of 'Louis' van Beethoven's Violin Concerto (above), includes the information that a piano version of the work is available.

present path, he and the public will come to no good end.

Perhaps the Concerto was too subtly original and too unusual for contemporary audiences used to showy, virtuoso concertos. It is, after all, a difficult composition of great poise, depth and beauty.

Publication and popularity

Beethoven's Violin Concerto was relatively slow to make its way into the concert repertoire. Two publishers, Pleyel in Paris and Simrock in Bonn, seem to have rejected it and it was in fact the London publisher Clementi who took the work in 1807. A few violinists attempted to establish it, but it was not until the 12-year-old Hungarian prodigy Joseph Joachim played it in 1844 in London, under the baton of the composer Mendelssohn, that the work really 'arrived'.

There is an interesting postscript to the story of the Violin Concerto. Beethoven made a piano arrangement of it – that is, with the solo part arranged for piano rather than violin. It was the London-based publisher Clementi who commissioned this version. And, remembering the composer's original inscription on the score ('Concerto par Clemenza pour Clement'), Clementi's involvement seems very appropriate. This is how Clementi announced the news in a letter:

I have at last made a compleat (sic) conquest of that haughty beauty, Beethoven . . . I agreed with him to take in mss. three quartets, a symphony, an

overture and a concerto for the violin, which is beautiful, and which at my request he will adapt for the pianoforte, for all of which we are to pay him two hundred pounds sterling.

The beauty and popularity of the Violin Concerto in its original form, however, have caused the piano arrangement to be almost entirely neglected by pianists, though Daniel Barenboim has recorded it. Beethoven thought well enough of it, however, to dedicate it to the young wife of Stephan von Breuning, Julie, whose husband had been the dedicatee of the original violin version.

Programme notes

First movement – Allegro ma non troppo (Cadenza: Fritz Kreisler)

The four quiet timpani strokes (evenly-spaced drum taps) that open Beethoven's Violin Concerto will prove to be highly significant throughout the first movement. They form a rhythmic, rather than melodic, ideal, in a way rather like the four-note motif that begins Beethoven's Fifth Symphony, though the pace and mood here are totally different.

These lead at once to a gentle *first subject* (first theme) played in a smooth curve of woodwind:

Example 1

The drum's taps and the melody are evidently both contrasted and complementary: masculine and feminine, bass and treble, rhythmic and melodic. The melody is answered straight away with the four repeated notes of the opening, only this time on the orchestral strings: if the music here seems to 'jolt' a bit, it is because an alien D sharp is introduced.

Now comes a series of fairly gently dipping and rising scales. Suddenly the pleasant pastoral mood is shattered by a violent orchestral outburst. It is worth noting this loud 'outburst' theme, which strides forward sternly, because it will play quite an important part in the first movement. After this things calm down – the first violins play alone at this point – and the second main theme of the movement, a sweet, lyrical melody, is introduced. Like the first theme (Example 1), it is played by

The overall mood of the Violin Concerto is one of tenderness and warmth – qualities conveyed with great sensitivity by Leonardo (left). This is especially true of the second movement.

Understanding music: the violin virtuoso

When Liszt dazzled audiences with his keyboard displays, he played brand new pianos, radically different from the pianos a dozen years earlier; when the violin virtuoso Niccolò Paganini played, he played, like most violin virtuosi since, on violins over 100 years old. The instrument reached a peak of perfection, never surpassed, in the hands of a few Italian master craftsmen, Antonio Stradivari and the Guarneri family, who were making violins between 1650 and 1750.

Of course, there were changes. As the patronage of the aristocracy declined, musicians began to rely more and more on concerts for financial support. So virtuoso violinists were forced to modify their Stradivaris and Guarneris, to make them powerful enough to be heard in large concert halls, by raising the bridge and using longer and heavier strings. They also began to use the taut, concave bow invented by François Tourte in 1785.

Naturally, then, violin technique had a long time to become established. During the 17th and 18th centuries, there were two main traditions of violin playing: the French style and the Italian style. The simpler, rhythmic French style harked back to the origins of the violin as a dance band instrument. The Italian style, on the other hand, was sophisticated and rhythmically freer, modelled on the human voice, and much more suited to displays of solo instrumental skill. Not surprisingly, most of the violin virtuosi up until 1750 were Italian – figures like Locatelli and the prolific Tartini, who wrote over 100 concertos for the violin.

Nevertheless, the French style did have something to offer the virtuoso, and the modern style developed, to some extent, from the marriage of both schools, stimulated in particular by the 'father of modern violin playing', Giovanni Viotti, an Italian virtuoso who moved to Paris in 1781. It was Viotti's French disciples, Kreutzer, Rode and especially Baillot who, through institutions like the new Paris Conservatoire, helped to establish the way in which modern violin technique was taught.

The new virtuoso style that emerged was heavily influenced by the need for power and brilliance in the concert hall. The Italian virtuoso style had depended upon subtleties in bowing, and the soft convex bow had allowed the player to give many 'nuances' in a single stroke. With the new style, and the tauter, heavier bow, bowing techniques were more dramatic, with strokes such as the *martelé* (giving a *sforzando,* an effect of strident attack) and the 'seamless' *legato* (long even strokes, moving smoothly between notes), but the subtle nuances disappeared – the subtleties of the new virtuoso style were in the fingering.

The effect of these changes can be seen clearly in the way the violin was held. With the new style, the left hand needed to be free for fingering effects, so violinists increasingly began to tuck the instrument under their chins for support – in the 1820s, Spohr introduced a proper chinrest.

The power and brilliance of the new style encouraged theatrical virtuoso displays, and it is not surprising that many violinists, particularly in Germany, rejected the technical wizardry inspired by Paganini's dazzling displays, feeling that musical ideals were being sacrificed to virtuosity. To some extent, violin technique split into two schools again; the French, who enjoyed technical bravura, and the Germans, led by Spohr, who emphasized musical values. Yet many of the great virtuosi were able to step across the divide – violinists like Joseph Joachim, Brahms's friend and one of the greatest players of the 19th century, were brought up in the German tradition but happily studied Paganini's Caprices. And by the end of the century, distinctions had blurred.

Joseph Joachim (1831–1907), the great virtuoso. Notice how the violin is held under the chin to give maximum scope to the left hand and power to the bow stroke.

the woodwind. Notice that it is accompanied lightly by the violins playing the drum-tap motif:

We hear this lovely theme first in the major and then (violins) the minor – a subtle change of mood. Yet another melodic idea follows on from this, and a tune which features the four repeated notes can be heard. This rather quiet, musing section is then swept aside by a triumphant, almost march-like passage for the whole orchestra, marked *fortissimo* (very loud).

The main themes of the exposition section have now been stated. Next, as this is a concerto, we are given a kind of repeat procedure in which the soloist makes his entrance to give us this first section again, but now in his own freer and more

Some of the loveliest passages of the Violin Concerto evoke a mood of stillness and mystery, very much like that in Claude's painting (below). At these moments, an atmosphere of almost hushed rapture is created.

Robert-Schumann-Haus, Zwickau

rhapsodic way. And so the solo violin emerges out of the orchestral texture climbing like a soaring bird into its high range. As the woodwind, with a kind of quiet restraint, play the first theme again, the violin above decorates it in a golden thread of sound. The exposition repeat continues – similar but by no means identical now the soloist is in command – and we find that the second theme (Example 2) is treated in the same way. It is introduced by a passage for the solo violin alone that ends in a sustained *trill* (the alternation of two adjacent notes) like a lark fluttering on high.

In the next passage of music more trills for the soloist, against the four-repeated-notes figure on the orchestral strings, lead in due course to the fortissimo 'outburst' theme from near the beginning of the movement, which the gentle tones of the violin seemed to have suppressed until now. Beethoven soon lets us hear a louder, more robust version of the gentle second theme (Example 2) as well. In fact, this considerable orchestral passage, in which the solo violin is silent, is predominantly loud.

Now the music subsides for the next entry of the soloist, as we move into the development section. Here Beethoven seems to muse on the melodies we have already heard, creating a quiet and mysterious world. The soloist, for example, after his rhapsodic entry climbs

The first page of the manuscript score of the Concerto (above), bears the inscription to Clement. Beethoven wrote the whole work very rapidly – according to his pupil, Czerny, pretty well 'straight through' – although he subsequently made some textual alterations.

up on high to give us a beautiful minor (not major as before) version of the first theme (Example 1). And all the time we hear that four-repeated-notes figure underpinning the music. At this point Beethoven, somewhat unconventionally, introduces a new theme altogether, now in the key of G minor. It is almost as if time had stopped: in a passage of great romance the soloist reflects on this beautiful melody – a melody which seems to have emerged utterly spontaneously.

Example 3

And then the mood changes abruptly. The full orchestra literally bangs out the four-note idea that began the Concerto (and has never been far away) and grandly restates the first theme (Example 1). This is now the *recapitulation* (or restatement of themes). The soloist is as eloquent and as lyrical as ever, and after the 'outburst' theme he plays the cadenza which leads us towards the end of this first movement.

As was the practice in Beethoven's time, the cadenza was a passage left for the soloist to improvise according to his taste. It was an opportunity for the virtuoso players of the day to display their technical prowess, while the orchestra and audience alike listened in respectful silence. Today, violinists always play a prepared cadenza, which in this performance is the one written by the great violinist Fritz Kreisler. After the cadenza, the orchestra gently comes in, and after a flourish, all is over.

The Violin Concerto's wonderfully joyful finale, with its dancing horns and vigorous orchestral accompaniment, suggests a boisterous country frolic (above).

Second movement – Larghetto

After the quite complex web of themes in the first movement, Beethoven now presents us with one basic melody in this slow and meditative Larghetto. (The instruction *larghetto* asks that the music be played in a slow, broadly expressive manner.) This beautiful theme is heard at once on the orchestral strings, muted and softened to mysteriously colour their tone. Then follows a series of thoughtful 'variations' – four of them to be precise. In these the theme is played by the orchestra and usually decorated by a rapturously high solo violin. The theme itself is full of pauses, which are filled by the soloist:

Example 4

In the first variation it is played by the clarinet (after the first few notes on the horn), in the second variation by the bassoon, and in the third variation by the orchestral violins (the soloist is silent here). Then there is an episode with a new, very beautiful melodic idea from the soloist. The fourth variation has the orchestral strings playing the theme *pizzicato* (plucked instead of bowed) and the soloist once again goes off on a sublime excursion; finally, what sounds like the beginning of yet another variation suddenly breaks off and leads without a break into the finale.

Third movement – Rondo (Allegro)

The final movement is vivid and joyful. Its one principal theme is heard, as is that of the Larghetto, at the very start. Rondo form, which Beethoven and other composers quite often chose for a concerto finale, has the main theme stated at key points in the movement and separated by episodes that provide contrast without breaking the overall mood.

The first episode here is best identified by the spontaneous dancing figure that accompanies it, played by the two orchestral horns. A brief return to the main theme, (with delicate solo violin and vigorous orchestral playing) leads to a smoother-flowing, quieter episode in the minor key (violin over sustained orchestral strings). Then we are back to the rhythmic main theme again, followed by a modified version of the first episode with the 'dancing horns'. Next, another cadenza – a short one this time. Then with the orchestra's quiet, almost hesitant reappearance, we rightly feel that we are approaching the end of this finale. But Beethoven has one more trick up his sleeve, and seems to have decided to end the movement quietly. But the last two chords are loud ones, like someone proudly announcing 'that's that!'

Fritz Kreisler

The violin cadenza described here, written by Fritz Kreisler, is one of several pieces he composed. The composition of this piece was no doubt influenced by his playing style which was very individual. He was unusual in that without much practice and in an undramatic manner he produced music of unaffected brilliance.

Born in Vienna in 1875, he showed early promise and received no further tuition beyond the age of 12 years. Following Kreisler's London début in May 1902, the English composer Elgar composed his Violin Concerto for him, which was premièred in 1910, with the composer conducting. It took him a while to gain fame because his style of fingering and bowing was ahead of its time. Not only did he use vibrato on long, sustained notes but also on very short notes, thus bringing to the music extra sparkle and life.

Great interpreters

Arthur Grumiaux (violinist)
Born in 1921, Arthur Grumiaux was the modern heir to a distinguished Belgian violin tradition. A student of Alfred Dubois, who himself was a pupil of the legendary Eugene Ysaÿe, Grumiaux soon gave clear signs of his prodigious talent. By 1939 he

was accomplished enough to win the Henri Vieuxtemps and François Prume prizes. Just prior to the German invasion of Belgium in 1940, he had finished off his music studies in Paris, where Georges Enesco was his composition teacher.

Immediately after the war he rapidly came to prominence in Europe as one of his generation's most gifted musicians. In 1949, he took over from his former teacher, Dubois, as professor of violin at the Brussels Conservatory. By the mid-50s his fame was established worldwide – not only in Europe and America, but also in Japan and the Far East. Since then, he steadily added to his stature with an extensive series of remarkable recordings. Arthur Grumiaux died in 1986.

Outstanding perhaps among his interpretations are his Beethoven, Bach and Mozart, and his recording of Alban Berg's violin concerto is a modern classic.

Concertgebouw, Amsterdam
Amsterdam's premier orchestra deserves to be rated high among Europe's finest. Formed in 1888, it was fortunate to have the brilliant Willem Mengelberg as conductor from 1895–1941. Examples of the orchestra's work under Mengelberg are still available on album. Under his leadership the orchestra quickly gained a distinguished reputation throughout Europe, and during this period virtually every major conductor and many leading

composers were guest leaders.

From 1941 to 1961 Eduard van Beinum led the orchestra in many distinguished concerts and recordings. Since 1961 the conducting post has been held by Bernard Haitink, first in partnership with Eugene Jochum, then solely since 1964. Since his appointment he has been recognized as one of the outstanding interpreters of today. His Mahler Symphony cycle, recorded with the Concertgebouw, is seen as a high-point in the orchestra's distinguished career. The Concertgebouw has become the mainstay of the Holland Festival, having given concerts every summer from 1947 to the present day.

The interpretation
Grumiaux and the Concertgebouw, under the guest conductor Sir Colin Davis, immediately establish an uncommon level of understanding in their interpretation of Beethoven's Concerto. The violinist's natural sense of balance and purity of line find a sensitive foil in the finely attuned orchestral accompaniment. The nobility of character inherent in this Concerto is vividly displayed for the listener, as well as Beethoven's characteristic striving for perfect construction and use of musical materials. It is often said of this piece that there is not a single unconsidered or unnecessary note. These fine artists demonstrate eloquently the truth of this observation.

FURTHER LISTENING

Beethoven orchestral works
Triple Concerto in C major, op. 56
The Triple Concerto, completed in 1805, was conceived in late 1803: thus it coincides with a number of other masterpieces such as the 'Eroica' Symphony, the 'Waldstein' Sonata and *Fidelio,* his only opera. That it clearly holds its own in this company testifies to its greatness. The work is in three movements, the first setting the style and tone of the rest. The main themes and variations are shared more or less equally by the soloists.
Romances nos. 1 and 2 for violin and orchestra, opp. 40 and 60.
These two simple and charming works are sometimes considered to be mere trifles, but that is to do their lyricism and sound construction scant justice. Intended pehaps by the composer as studies for slow concerto movements, they exhibit great poise and are quite self-contained.
Egmont – Overture, op. 84
This overture is the most significant portion of the incidental music written for an 1810 revival of Goethe's play. In it, Beethoven combines the themes which he saw as the essence of the play's meaning – the clash of good and evil.

Symphony no.5 in C minor, op.67

This dynamic symphony represents one of Beethoven's greatest achievements. Driven on by an irresistible energy, the music sweeps the listener along from the menacing opening to a triumphant conclusion.

The arresting opening bars of Beethoven's Fifth Symphony must be some of the most memorable in all music. Beethoven himself supposedly alluded to these four violent hammer blows in his famous remark 'Thus fate knocks at the door', though this was made many years after the symphony was written. Nearer the time, according to his friend and pupil Czerny, he simply attributed the inspiration for the opening notes to a yellow-hammer's song which he had heard when strolling through the Praterpark in Vienna.

Not surprisingly, audiences have preferred the 'Fate' myth to Czerny's story, as it accords perfectly with the dynamic nature of the symphony. The unremitting drive of the first movement depicts a dramatic conflict which only finds resolution in the heroic finale, and which has caught the public imagination ever since it was first performed.

The first performance

The first performance took place on 22 December 1808, at the Theater an der Wien, in a concert which by present day standards seems gargantuan. First came the Sixth Symphony ('Pastoral'), which was also receiving its first performance; the aria, 'Ah Perfido', part of the Mass in C, and the Third Piano Concerto – it was to have been the new Fourth Concerto but the pianist was unable to learn that work in the short time given him to study. Then in the second half the Symphony in C minor – listed then as number Six but which has ever since been known as the Fifth – another movement from the C major Mass, and finally the Fantasia for piano, chorus and orchestra, whose piano introduction Beethoven apparently improvised on the spot. This marathon concert began at half past six and continued for four hours in a freezing cold hall: 'There we sat from 6.30 until 10.30 in the bitter cold,' wrote Reichardt, the composer and journalist, 'and found from experience that one could have too much even of a good thing . . .'

It is hardly surprising that the standard of the performances left much to be desired, for it seems that Beethoven's fiery temper had antagonized the orchestra, and they only agreed to rehearse if he did not remain in the hall. He was therefore banished to an ante-room, where, in what

must have been desperate frustration, coupled with his deafness, he had extreme difficulty following what was going on, only being kept in touch by visits from the orchestra leader, Seyfried. However, he does seem to have conducted the actual concert himself.

Contemporary reports of that evening seem to concentrate more on a mishap which occurred during the performance of the Choral Fantasia, when the orchestra ground to a halt over a misunderstanding in the wind section. An exasperated Beethoven flew from his piano to try to sort the problem out, while the long-suffering audience waited for the concert to restart. Reichardt, however, does refer to 'a great symphony, very elaborate and too long'. Perhaps by this time the audience had found the whole occasion rather too much.

Critical reaction

Nevertheless, when the work was played in Leipzig in 1810, E. T. A. Hoffman, writing in the *Allgemeine Musikalische Zeitung*, the leading musical journal of the day, described the new symphony as 'one of the most important works of the master, whose foremost position among instrumental composers probably no one would now dispute', and finishes by describing the work as 'a concept of genius executed with profound deliberation, which in a very high degree brings the romantic content of the music to expression'.

On the other hand, the composer Spohr, discussing a performance of the symphony in Munich in 1815, felt that 'with all its individual beauties it does not form a classical whole,' and found the famous opening phrase 'wanting in the dignity which to my mind is indispensable for the opening of a symphony'.

The new work reached London at a concert by the Philharmonic Society on 15 April, 1816, where the simplicity of the opening bars seems to have provoked gales of laughter among the musicians of the orchestra during the rehearsal. The Society, however, performed it every year for the next 55 years.

The process of composition

As always with Beethoven the gestation period of composition on this symphony was a long one. The first ideas appear in

Beethoven portrayed at about the age of 34, when he had just begun work on the Fifth. Ideas appear in sketches dated April, 1804, but the symphony wasn't completed until 1808.

Fate – embodied in Michelangelo's stern image of the Creator (right) – is thought to be the enigmatic theme of this extraordinarily powerful composition.

Beethoven's sketchbooks as early as 1804, alongside similar sketches which found their way into the Fourth Piano Concerto. Yet further ideas appear at the end of the sketchbooks for the Third Symphony ('Eroica'), which was finished and first performed in 1805. This symphony, which is much longer than the great symphonies by Haydn or Mozart and tremendous in the impact of its musical content, had revealed to the musical public the dynamic and revolutionary nature of Beethoven's music.

It is probable that the Fifth Symphony was intended as successor to the rugged

'Eroica', but Beethoven's attentions were temporarily diverted by his relationship with the Countess Theresa of Brunswick, who had been his pupil for several years. During 1806 he worked on the lighter Fourth Symphony, a work which no doubt reflects his happier frame of mind. But he took up work again in 1807 and completed the Fifth Symphony either later that year or early in 1808. Strangely, during this period he was working simultaneously on the charming and lyrical 'Pastoral' Symphony.

To us, hearing the final result, the Fifth seems to grow in an utterly spontaneous manner from one idea to the next, yet it

had caused Beethoven a great deal of trouble. Even the famous hammer-blow opening went through several transformations before he arrived at the utterly simple and emphatic statement with which the symphony begins.

Musical influences

Beethoven's genius was so individual that we frequently tend to overlook the influence upon him of his great predecessors. Haydn's vast series of 104 symphonies, begun in 1755 and completed in 1795, had developed the form of the symphony from a simple serenade – a harmonious composi-

tion divided into different stylized dance forms – to the complex, more personal works of his later years. As his former pupil, Beethoven must have been very familiar with these. Also influential were the works of Bach's most famous son, Carl Philip Emmanuel Bach, whose music has a dramatic cut and thrust which is quite individual, and whose keyboard works helped shape the style of Beethoven's piano sonatas. Mozart's great symphonies were also looked to as a source of inspiration.

But in this Fifth Symphony Beethoven is not really breaking old moulds and creating a new form. In fact the form of the first

68

movement is not only conventional, as far as any precedent had been set in the previous 50 years by either Haydn or Mozart, but, like the great classical compositions, is perfectly balanced in its division into four equal parts: the *exposition* – the opening section in which the musical themes are set out – lasts for 124 bars, the *development* – in which these themes are expanded and explored – 123 bars, the *recapitulation* – basically a variation on the opening section – 126 bars, and the *coda* – simply the concluding section (coda is the Italian word for 'tail') – 129 bars. Rather it is the originality of ideas contained within this strict formal plan, the brightness of the inspiration and the energy of the music that were new.

Programme notes

The Fifth Symphony is frequently described in warlike terms – heroism, conflict and triumph. Yet the conflict is generally considered to be a personal rather than an external one: the struggle between the physical world, which in Beethoven's case included his advancing deafness and growing frustrations, and the inner sound world of tonal images coupled with his concept of God.

The symphony is divided into four movements: an *Allegro con brio* (meaning lively and with verve) which moves at a very brisk pace; an *Andante con moto* (walking pace, with animation) a steady,

flowing movement; another Allegro, traditionally known as the *Scherzo* (meaning vigorous and playful in character), which leads into the final movement, also an Allegro, by way of a long transitional passage, which Berlioz, the famous French composer, found absolutely stunning.

First movement – Allegro con brio

Example 1

Beethoven begins the symphony by throwing down the grandiose challenge. 'Thus fate knocks at the door', but neither this

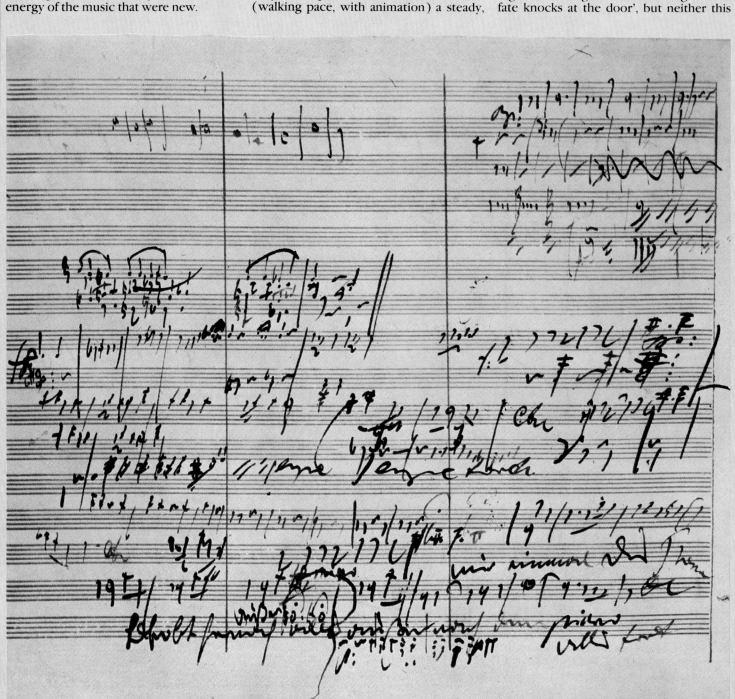

69

Count Razumovsky (above) shared the dedication for the Fifth Symphony with Prince Lobkowitz (above right). Both men were great music lovers and enthusiastic patrons of Beethoven's art.

Beethoven's numerous sketches for the Fifth Symphony (left), show that a great deal of effort as well as inspiration went into its composition. Even the opening bars – stunning in their apparent simplicity – underwent several painstaking transformations.

Beethoven told his pupil Czerny that the opening bars of the Fifth were inspired by the rhythmic pattern of the yellow-hammer's song.

famous four-note motto nor its repetition a tone lower down tells us the key of the symphony. It is not until after the phrase has been repeated several times by the strings that the full orchestra establishes the key of C minor. The full orchestra here means two each of flutes, oboes, clarinets, bassoons, horns, trumpets, plus timpani and strings. Constant repetition of this phrase, builds up magnificently towards a powerful climax.

The mood then changes with the introduction of a new, gentler theme on the violins and woodwind, more flowing and lyrical than the opening, but still with that hammer-blow phrase sounding in the bass, and which again through constant repetition builds up to another great climax and brings the first section to a close. Because of the very terseness of this opening, it seems completely natural that it should be repeated before proceeding from the exposition section to the exploration of these musical ideas in the development section.

The horns and clarinets once again give out the main theme with great force, and the music charges on with unstoppable and irresistible energy, still repeating over and over the little phrase, while the moving harmonies give a distinct feeling of unrest as if anticipating a storm. Strings and wind instruments alternate in sequences in a passage of extraordinary tension, and then for a short period the energy seems to be spent, only to return with added force when Beethoven forcefully drums home his 'Fate' theme, this time using the sound of the full orchestra, as we pass into the recapitulation.

But now occurs one of Beethoven's great masterstrokes. The music suddenly relaxes its unremitting energy, and a solo oboe gives out a strange lyrical cry. Is this the 'still small voice' that is at the centre of all creation? Beethoven's own creed, adopted from an Egyptian temple inscription, was on his desk when he worked: 'I am that which

is, I am everything that is, that was, and that will be. No mortal man has raised my veil. He is himself alone, and it is to this aloneness that all things owe their being.' This brief, poignant oboe solo, suddenly making itself heard amid the tumult, is surely a musical expression of that 'aloneness'.

But immediately, the pounding energy starts up again mounting to another grand climax. Just before the second, lyrical theme reappears, the 'Fate' theme is played loudly by the horn section.

The concluding section, the coda, which occupies the last part of this movement, contains still further development of the opening phrase, driven to the final climax with incessant, almost demonic energy. This first movement has long been regarded as one of the great miracles of music. Berlioz said it revealed Beethoven's 'most private griefs, his fiercest wrath, his most lonely and desolate meditations, his midnight visions, his bursts of enthusiasm'. Yet all this is expressed with that tiny 'Fate theme' repeated hundreds of times, and with a passion and fire that overwhelm everything in their path.

Second movement – Andante con moto

The second movement is in complete contrast to the fiery energy of the first. It is a series of variations on a long, stately melody which starts on the violas and cellos and gradually unfolds in several directions. Violas and cellos are soon joined by the woodwind and the upper strings, and then the addition of the brass bring it to a triumphant peak. But within this theme is embedded the rhythm of the 'Fate' theme from the first movement, now greatly slowed down but present in the second limb of this long melody, heard first on clarinets and bassoons, and then with full force on the horns and trumpets.

Example 2

In the first variation, violas and cellos weave a chain of notes about the theme, which rises once again to a powerful statement on the brass. A strange and mysterious change of mood follows, beneath which cellos reiterate an ominous rhythm, which acts as a bridge to the second variation. The running notes now double their speed, while the accompanying chords only hint at the framework of the theme, and, as the whole orchestra joins in, all but obliterate the running notes in cellos and basses.

There is now a pause in the flow of the music, while in the third variation Beethoven indulges in some whimsical variants for woodwind on the opening notes of his theme, before the whole orchestra returns *fortissimo* (very loudly) with the second half of the theme. Another pause occurs while Beethoven again plays around with those four notes. But this capriciousness is swept aside for a last full grandiose statement of the main theme. A most beautiful and touching moment on strings, achieved by the slightest alteration to the melody, interrupts, but Beethoven soon banishes this to bring the movement to a calmly triumphant close.

Third movement – Allegro (Scherzo)

The last two movements are run together without a break, as was the practice of the time. The third movement returns to the main key of the symphony and is traditionally referred to as the *Scherzo* – literally Italian for 'joke'. But the quiet, mysterious opening, whose theme seems like a ghostly memory of the finale of Mozart's 40th Symphony, does not seem particularly humorous: the Mozart theme does appear in Beethoven's sketchbook adjacent to this scherzo theme, so the resemblance is not coincidental. The air is cleared by the horns boldly giving out a theme fortissimo, whose relationship to the first movement's 'Fate' motif is obvious:

Example 3

Beethoven continues to work on these two contrasting themes at some length.

The middle section of this movement is more scherzo-like in character. Cellos and basses set off a busy, bumbling motive which frequently cuts across the main theme in a vigorous, lively rhythm. For a few brief seconds at the end of this passage, the woodwind affectionately transform this theme into a charming lyrical idea, before the mysterious opening returns. But now, Beethoven, against all formal procedures, maintains this atmosphere, not repeating the opening of the movement. The violins play the second theme *pizzicato* – where the strings are plucked rather than bowed – and an atmosphere of almost comic expectancy pervades the music. There is a long-held note above which the violins wander, which seems to hint that something significant is about to happen.

The music gradually grows louder and louder in an enormous *crescendo* and then, in triumphant style, the heroic finale arrives. What is more, the orchestra has suddenly grown in size: a piccolo, double bassoon, and, most impressively, three trombones, add to the clamour. This is the first time that trombones had been used in the concert hall; Mozart had introduced them into the opera house for the damnation scene of *Don Giovanni* in 1787, but it was Beethoven who added them to the symphony orchestra.

Fourth movement – Allegro

The finale is a great march of triumph, and one can perfectly well understand the French soldier who, on hearing this symphony for the first time, leapt to his feet during this ceremonial blaze of sound crying, 'C'est l'Empereur'. But is this triumph a military one, despite the martial terms in which Beethoven expresses it? Our 'Fate' motif is still present in the clamour, but now transformed into a dancing melody – only the rhythm remains. Perhaps the triumph that Beethoven is depicting here is the ultimate personal triumph

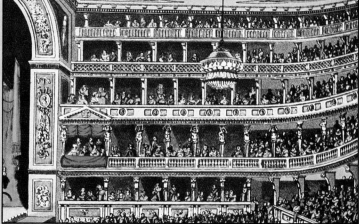

The magnificent Theater an der Wien (right and below), where the Fifth Symphony was first performed on the 22 December, 1808. The programme consisted of four hours of music, the concert-hall was bitterly cold, the orchestra ill-rehearsed and out of tune. All in all, the Fifth Symphony didn't have quite the impact that it now invariably commands.

The poet and musician, E. T. A. Hoffmann (left), had a real understanding of the Fifth Symphony. Writing about it in 1810, he drew attention to the way in which the entire first movement is built up from one small but inspired idea: 'There is no simpler idea than that on which the composer based the entire Allegro, and we see with admiration how he succeeded in using rhythm to link all the subsidiary ideas to that theme, so that they serve only to unfold more and more the character of the whole, which the theme could only hint at.'

A romantic image of Beethoven in the process of composing (below). Slumped over the piano, utterly exhausted by his mental exertions, he is surrounded by the many spirits that people his inner world – spirits of torment as well as of inspiration.

of the fully realized human being, reconciled with his fate and at one with God.

New ideas pour out in this final movement in generous profusion. First the triumphant hymn on the now-enlarged orchestra, soon followed by a leaping theme on the horns, then the dance-like theme and yet another hymn-like theme, which itself has the 'Fate' motif embedded in it, somewhat quieter at first but soon matching the preceding themes in its power and grandeur.

Example 4

Beethoven here asks for the whole of this section to be repeated, although later in the 19th century it became traditional to cut this repeat and go straight into the development.

A great deal is made of the dance theme in the first part of the development, throwing it around from one instrument to another, and building it into a climax of tremendous force, when suddenly everything comes to a halt. Here occurs another of Beethoven's great masterstrokes, for he reintroduces a ghostly echo of the theme from the third movement (Example 3). 'Fate' is still present, and, as at the end of the Scherzo, it exists in the insistent repetition of one chord, although this time without the colourful wanderings of the violins in the string section.

Now all the themes of triumph return and are developed at length to produce an effect of boundless energy and joy. The final section starts with a variant of the leaping horn theme, and with a gradual increase of speed we rush headlong into the final pages, with the hymn-like theme (Example 4) played at tremendous speed.

What possible resolution could there be to all this joyous energy other than the final 29 bars based entirely on the triumphant C major chord? This ending has seemed like overstatement to many musicians, and yet, if the performance has been one that has fully realized the passion and excitement of Beethoven's score, then this thundering reiteration can be the only possible ending to Beethoven's triumphant hymn of faith.

Later interpretations

Ever since it was written this symphony has been a favourite for both audiences and conductors throughout the world. In France, François-Antoine Habeneck was one of its earliest interpreters, although Berlioz castigated him for omitting the repeat in the last movement. It was possibly at one of his performances that the famous singer Malibran first heard the work, and was so overwhelmed by it that she had a fit of convulsions and had to be carried from the concert hall.

Wagner adjusted the bassoon part for the horns in the first movement, and obviously indulged in great exaggerations of Beethoven's markings, if his comments on performance are anything to go by. 'The life blood of the note must be squeezed out of it to the last drop, with force enough to arrest the waves of the sea and lay bare the ground of the ocean,' all this and more about the fourth note of the score!

More recent interpretations have been content to follow Beethoven's original scoring, finding it rich in drama and immensely powerful as it stands, without extra instrumental parts.

FURTHER LISTENING

Symphony no. 3 in E flat major, ('Eroica')
With the Third Symphony, Beethoven pointed the way forward for the symphonic form, rather than using earlier composers as his musical models. It is much longer than any of the great classical symphonies, in order to accommodate his wide-ranging and prophetic ideas. Heroic and revolutionary in character, its original dedication to Napoleon was removed by a disillusioned Beethoven.

Symphony no. 6 in F major, ('Pastoral')
Written at the same time as the Fifth, the playful and lyrical Sixth Symphony is a remarkable contrast in character. Unusually for Beethoven, it was written as a description of ideas which lie outside the music itself. The symphony is a celebration of rural existence, each movement illustrating a different aspect of country life.

Symphony no. 9 in D minor, ('Choral')
The Ninth is the most large-scale and fully-developed exposition of Beethoven's symphonic ideas, and is commonly regarded as one of the world's greatest masterpieces. Beethoven boldly decided to incorporate human voices into the finale.

Understanding music: what is a symphony?

Nowadays, the word 'symphony' is often used to describe any large orchestral work, just as the symphony orchestra can play a whole range of orchestral pieces as well as symphonies. But in the Classical and Romantic eras, its meaning was much more specific. Then, as now, the symphony was a work for a large orchestra, but it was simply one variation of a musical form called the *sonata* and it is the sonata tradition that provides the key to understanding the symphony.

The sonata strongly influenced Romantic music – many great composers wrote music in this idiom. But it is not always easy to identify a sonata because a piece written in this idiom may be called by a wide variety of names. A sonata for five instruments, for instance, may be called a *quintet:* a sonata for eight instruments may be called an *octet.* The symphony is essentially a sonata for a full orchestra – but if the work is written for soloist and orchestra, it may be called a *concerto.*

During the 18th century, the sonata developed a more clearly defined structure, so that by the time of Beethoven, sonatas nearly always had three or four distinct sections or *movements.* The use of movements allowed the composer to include a wide range of, moods within a single piece. With three movements, the first was generally the longest, but it was also fairly fast *(allegro)*; the second was slow and lyrical; and the last movement was stirring and vivacious.

Early symphonies tended to have this three-movement structure, but during Haydn's lifetime (1732–1809), an extra movement was added, usually coming either second or third. This movement was generally based on a dance called the *minuet* which was very popular in the ballrooms of the time.

The long first movement of the symphony is almost invariably rousing and lively, serving as a fanfare to make the audience sit up and listen. But it is almost always broader in conception

and scope than any of the other movements. A range of moods from fierce drama to lyrical sadness may come within a single movement.

The structure

Naturally, the long first movement of a symphony has the most elaborate structure, called *sonata form.* Sonata form has three main sections: *exposition, development* and *recapitulation.* In the exposition, the composer uses two main tunes or themes, called *subjects.* Usually, the two main subjects contrast in mood, the first being brisk and powerful, the second more gentle. Often there is a short *bridge* between the two subjects. In the development, the composer develops the themes of the exposition. And in the recapitulation, the music returns to the themes of the exposition, slightly modified. Many composers would also add a slow introductory piece to the movement and a brisk tailpiece or *coda.*

The second movement of the

symphony is usually slow and lyrical and it is often the place where the most enchanting melodies occur. The structure is generally very simple — indeed it has to be, since anything complex would go on too long. They are often like songs in structure, opening with one tune, changing to a new key for another tune and then returning to the original key to play the first tune again.

The dance movement was originally a pair of dances, a *minuet* and a *trio,* which is a type of minuet. Beethoven speeded up the movement and called it a *scherzo* — literally, a 'joke' — but it is still dance music. Other composers had composed 'fun' music before Beethoven, but Beethoven was the first to include a scherzo in a symphony. It was so successful that virtually every composer who has written four-movement symphonies has since Beethoven included a scherzo.

In many ways the final movement is similar to the first and is often in a

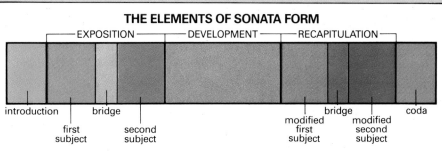

THE ELEMENTS OF SONATA FORM

EXPOSITION ——— DEVELOPMENT ——— RECAPITULATION

introduction   bridge   bridge   coda
          first   second   modified   modified
          subject   subject   first   second
                                                        subject   subject

The first movement of a symphony is usually in sonata form. This has three main parts: the exposition, the development and the recapitulation.

simplified sonata form. But it was traditional for a symphony to end on a happy note in Beethoven's time — sad endings, such as Tchaikovsky's 'Pathétique', came later. So the finale, like the third movement, was often based on a dance.

Today this elaborate structure seems rather restrictive, but Classical and Romantic composers produced a

remarkable diversity of music within this format. The later symphonies of Beethoven are startlingly different from Haydn's; those of Brahms bear little resemblance to Mozart's. While some composers continued to work within the traditional structure, others abandoned it altogether. Symphonic form was not static but broadened in scope throughout the Classical and Romantic eras.

In the background

Scientists still argue which contributes most to our personalities, talents and behaviour: the inheritance of our genes or the influence of our environment. However, it is undeniable that we cannot help being affected to some extent by our surroundings, both in the narrow sense of our personal backgrounds and in the global sense of the times we live in. Great composers are no exception, and the following pages describe the historical background to Beethoven's life and how political, cultural and scientific events influenced and inspired him: the renaissance in German art that took place at the turn of the 18th century; the rise to power, imperial reign and fall of Napoleon Bonaparte; the power of the House of Hapsburg that dominated central Europe from the imperial capital of Vienna where Beethoven spent much of his life; and the scientific developments that took place in medicine during the 19th century to transform the crude and ineffective treatments known to and suffered by the unfortunate Beethoven.

IN THE BACKGROUND

German Romanticism

Napoleon Bonaparte

The achievements of Beethoven in music were paralleled by contemporary developments in German literature, painting and philosophy – as can be seen in the works of Goethe and Schiller, of Friedrich and of Kant. This late-18th-century flowering of German culture is usually described as Romantic and involved a new attitude towards the creative artist. Instead of being a virtual servant of the privileged, the artist would use his unique insight to guide the people through the revolutionary upheavals of the times. At first, Napoleon Bonaparte, who rose from humble beginnings to lead the citizen armies of France against its monarchical enemies, seemed the archetypal Romantic hero. However, Beethoven and other artists were disillusioned when Napoleon seized power to make himself Emperor and to destroy the infant French republic.

'The spiritual eye'

The haunting landscapes of Friedrich, the heroic panoramas of Koch and the spiritual allegories of Runge reflect in exciting and original ways the dramatic developments in German Romantic music.

Mozart, Beethoven and Schubert are well known to us. What we tend to overlook at times is that the works of these great composers form part of a rich flowering that ranged throughout the arts and sciences in the German-speaking countries. German culture was undergoing a rebirth around 1800 which seemed to affect almost every aspect of human achievement. Apart from music, this can be seen most strikingly in philosophy, where Kant opened up crucial new avenues of thought, and in literature, where Goethe dominated the contemporary European field.

The visual arts played a full part in these developments. While not quite as rich in achievement as the music, philosophy and literature of the period, they reflected many of the same interests in original and exciting ways. Furthermore, there was one painter, at least, who was of the first rank. This was the landscape artist Caspar David Friedrich. Born four years later than Beethoven, his art came to maturity at the time when that composer was writing his most celebrated concertos and symphonies. The two never met. Nor do they appear to have shown any particular interest in each other's work. Yet they often seem close in their attitudes, and sometimes in the effects that their creations produce. The sense of individualism, fascination with innovation, with the heroic, and with an

1 (above) Carstens: 'Night with her Children Sleep and Death'. Chalk. *The subject for this design was taken from the Greek poet Hesiod, and the figures are endowed with the still nobility of classical sculpture. For the great writer Goethe, Carstens was the artist 'with whom one gladly begins the new epoch of German art'.*

2 (above right) Koch: 'Schmadribach Falls'. Watercolour. *Koch, like Carstens, had a heroic vision, which he expressed through his gift for landscape painting. His celebrated Alpine scene is conceived on a grand scale, and reflects Carstens' view that high mountains inspire similar sensations to a Michelangelo.*

intense, near-mystical appreciation of nature – all these are tendencies that they share with each other and with many of their contemporaries.

Heroic genius

Perhaps the attitude that is most commonly found among artists at this time is the new view of creative genius. We are all familiar with the hackneyed image of the Romantic artist – unkempt, obsessed with his own greatness, living outside the conventions of society, and scorning the 'philistine' public. Nowadays, such an image is often used as a mask for mediocrity. But at the time when it first emerged, around 1800, it provided a genuine release. In the frightening and exciting decades that followed the French Revolution of 1789, it seemed that the artist had a new and important role to play. No longer was

Kupferstichkabinett, Basle/Archiv für Kunst und Geschichte

Kunsthalle, Hamburg

he to be a 'servant', performing duties for Church, monarchy and the privileged. Using his unique gifts he could stimulate awareness and provide guidance to people at a time when many of the traditional supports seemed to have rotted away.

In Germany, this image of the artist was crystallized most succinctly by the poet Friedrich Schiller. Throughout his career, Schiller used his powers as a writer to promote the image of a responsible and honourable society, and oppose the kind of feudal oppression that he himself had suffered as a youth. His attitude aroused much support. Beethoven subscribed to it when he incorporated the poet's *Ode to Joy* – with its stirring phrase 'all men will become brothers' – into the final movement of his Ninth Symphony. Schiller also discussed his views in theoretical writings. The most

influential of these was his *Letters on the Aesthetic Education of Mankind* (1795). Written at a time when the 'Reign of Terror' that followed the Revolution in France was at its height, these letters asked the question of what value was art for people in a time of political crisis. The answer that Schiller gave was that people could only achieve true and responsible political freedom when they had developed the sense of judgement that comes with an appreciation of beauty. It was the duty of the artist to provide society with uplifting creations that would stimulate such awareness.

In the visual arts, the person who seemed to embody Schiller's ideal most completely was the North German, Asmus Jacob Carstens (1754–98). The son of a miller who was orphaned at the age of 15, Carstens struggled against tremendous odds to realize his ambition of becoming an artist. He had to endure seven years as an apprentice cooper before he could begin his art studies. From the start he wanted to be a 'history' painter – one who depicted important subjects, usually of a morally uplifting kind, using grand, idealized figures. He believed – like most other people of the day – that such an artist could only succeed if he based his art on the noble,

3 (above) Runge: 'Morning'. (Small version). Oil. *Runge rejected the 'heroic' vision of painters like Carstens and Koch in favour of an imagery of a more spiritual kind. This colour sketch is part of a series that Runge planned, but never completed, showing the 'Times of Day'. The tiny child lying in the dewy fields immediately recalls the infant Christ. With arms outstretched, in a gesture of rapture, he receives the gift of light – the liberator of the soul. Above him hovers the beautiful figure of Aurora, the bringer of dawn, whose spirits scatter rosebuds on the ground.*

classical forms of ancient Greek and Roman sculpture and the paintings of the great artists of the Italian Renaissance like Raphael and Michelangelo Buonarroti, who both worked in Rome. He therefore determined to go to Rome, where he could study such art at first hand.

He set out to walk there from North Germany – but had to give up when he got to northern Italy because of lack of funds. He was 38 before he was financed by the Berlin Academy, who supported him on the understanding that he would return after two years to teach for them. However, when this time was up he refused to come back, declaring, 'I do not belong to the Berlin Academy, but to mankind, which has a right to demand the highest possible development of my capabilities . . . .' In the years of life that remained to him he stayed in Rome, working in the midst of the art of his idols. He never received the commissions he craved for, to do vast paintings on the scale of Michelangelo's *Last Judgement*. All he left behind him were some modest oil paintings, and a large quantity of designs for the pictures that he would have liked to have made.

Some of these drawings, however, do convey in a most moving way the heroic qualities that he felt to be at the core of great art. His *Night with her Children Sleep and Death* (illustration 1) depicts a group of mythological characters as described by the Ancient Greek poet Hesiod. The figures are powerful, yet calm and balanced. Their grandeur is given poignancy by the pathos of the theme. Night, sleep and death are concepts that arouse feelings of meditation, fatalism and sadness. By clothing them in noble forms, Carstens seems to be implying that human dignity can be maintained even in the face of the frightening and the unknown.

Carstens' idealism, and his legendary intransigence, made him a focal point for other German artists who sought to paint heroic works. Closest to him was Joseph Anton Koch (1768–1839), a Tyrolese painter who arrived in Rome in 1795, after having broken away from the rigorous academic training in the Karlsschule in Stuttgart. For some years Koch continued Carstens' work in a direct way. He even made etchings after his hero's designs. After 1800, however, he turned increasingly away from figure painting and developed instead his gift for landscape painting. Carstens' sense of grandeur can be felt in a most stimulating way in many of these. Koch became one of the leading exponents in Rome of a new 'heroic' landscape, in which the classical compositions of the great 17th-century landscape painters – notably Claude Lorrain and Nicolas Poussin – were revised in the interests of a more vigorous, muscular kind of scenery. His most celebrated work is the mountain view. *The*

4 (left) Runge: 'The Huelsenbeck Children'. Oil.
Runge never liked portraiture, he considered it a trivial genre. However, his portraits are some of the most penetrating of his times. This painting shows the children of his brother's business partner with an almost disturbing directness. They are vigorous creatures of instinct; one brandishes a whip, another clutches at a leaf, only the older girl acts as a restraining influence. Their figures are made even more vital and monumental by Runge's use of scale. He places us at the children's level, underneath the towering sunflower.

Gemäldegalerie, Dresden/Deutsche Fotothek, Dresden

5 (left) Kersting: 'Caspar David Friedrich in his Studio'. Oil.
Friedrich was the greatest of the German Romantic painters. For him, landscape elements were symbols of the spiritual world: standing quietly before a blank canvas in his bare studio, he would only begin work when the image 'stood lifelike in his mind's eye'.

6 (below) Friedrich: 'Cross in the Mountains'. Oil.
This startling painting – an altarpiece for a private chapel – caused an uproar when it was first exhibited. One critic called it 'a veritable presumption if landscape painting were to sneak into the church and creep onto the altar'.

Schmadribach Falls amidst the Alps. The water-colour sketch (illustration 2) gives some idea of its scale. Painted in 1811, just a few years after Beethoven's Third Symphony, the *Eroica*, it is itself a kind of heroic symphony of nature, conveying a sense of the vastness and power of natural creation. It surveys a large expanse of Koch's native alpine scenery, moving from silent, snow-capped mountains to bare rocks and a torrential waterfall; and then below to dense woodlands, pasture and a gentle mountain stream. All these different moods are held together by the firmness of the design and the precision with which each form is depicted. It is in this sense of controlled immensity that Carstens' influence is perhaps most strongly felt.

Nature and mysticism

Both Carstens and Koch represented the new 'heroic' form of artistic vision. However, they were still quite traditional in the way they used classical forms to embody their ideas. And younger artists were beginning to find such imagery irrelevant: 'We are no longer Greeks and Romans, and when we contemplate their perfect works of art we can no longer feel the totality in the way that they did.' The man who wrote this was the painter Philipp Otto Runge (1777–1810). As his words suggest, he felt the perfection of the classical world to have little relevance for the modern era. Instead he sought to achieve an uplifting image using the more complex and intangible sensations that he felt epitomized the present age.

Like Carstens, Runge was an artist who never realized his grand ambitions. He died of tuberculosis at the age of 33 with only a fragment of his scheme completed. Like Carstens, too, he had some difficulties in establishing his career. Coming from a merchant family in the North-German Pomeranian town of Wolgast, he was 22 before he could gain his parents' permission to study to be an artist. The obscurity and originality of his ideas meant that he received little patronage. For most of his life he was largely dependent upon the generosity of his brother Daniel, a merchant in Hamburg.

Runge's ideas came to maturity while he was studying at Dresden between 1801 and 1804. It was here that he came into contact with a group of writers and critics who were seeking to turn away from classical models. One of their number, the critic Friedrich Schlegel, was the first to use the word 'romantic' to define the modern age. It was an age, he felt, that lacked the perfection of the classical world, but was more dynamic, and richer in spiritual potential. For Runge, the ecstatic feelings that he experienced before nature gave the most vivid intimations of this state. His cycle of the *Times of Day* – which was to include representations of Morning, Evening, Midday and Night – was intended to communicate a sense of the mystery and inner harmony of creation. Although he made designs for all four pictures, only one, *Morning,* came anywhere near completion. The coloured sketch for it (illustration 3) can give some idea of his objectives.

The picture shows a sunrise over a flat North-German plain. It is no ordinary sunrise, however, for the scene is peopled with allegorical figures. On the ground, in the foreground, lies a small child – reminiscent of the infant Christ – who opens out his arms to receive the gift of light. The place where the sun should be is dominated by the classical figure of

Aurora – the bringer of dawn. Around her are scattered small *genii* (spirits). Some of them bear rose petals – classical symbols of the dawn – to earth. The picture is surrounded by a frame in which pure white lilies are shown being brought to flower by the effects of light.

Light is, in fact, the unifying force in this complex picture. This point can perhaps be brought out most clearly if one compares it with Koch's *Schmadribach Falls.* Koch's heroic scene is based upon an actual place, and its effect depends upon the clear delineation of form. Runge's picture relies upon the realism of its light effects to conjure up a specific point in time, the moment at which light floods onto the earth and darkness is dispelled. It is typical of Runge that he should associate this moment with the birth of Christ. For he shared the belief of the Dresden Romantics that it was Christianity which had brought a new era of spiritual awareness.

While Runge's work is evidently a fantasy, it is based upon the most careful and probing study of natural effects. His diligence also made him an exceptionally fine portraitist, as such works as his *Huelsenbeck Children* (illustration 4) show. Runge disliked painting portraits – it seemed to him to be too menial and mundane a task. He never worked as a professional portraitist, but he did occasionally do pictures of his family and friends. The Huelsenbeck children were the offspring of a business colleague of his brother Daniel. He shows them playing in their garden. The baby grasps instinctively at a leaf, the boy rushes impulsively forward. Only the girl shows any concern for others, as she looks back towards the baby. They are in no way sentimentalized, but are shown as elemental, animal-like forces at one with the world of nature.

7 (above) Schinkel: 'Gothic Cathedral by a River'. Oil. *Schinkel, an important Prussian architect, developed an interest in landscape painting following the impact of Friedrich. Here, the Gothic cathedral, darkly silhouetted against a luminous sky, is intended as a political symbol of national regeneration.*

Caspar David Friedrich (1774–1840)

Runge's achievements – like those of Carstens – remained fragmentary. His visionary approach to nature was shared by another artist, however, who had a long and fulfilled career.

Like Runge, Friedrich came from the extreme north of Germany – in his case the Pomeranian town of Griefswald. Like Runge, too, it was his contact with the self-styled 'Romantics' in Dresden that brought about the development of his art. He went there in 1799 – after having studied at Copenhagen Academy – and was to remain based there for the rest of his life.

Friedrich's belief in the 'inner' vision of the artist is made clear in his advice to painters: 'Close your bodily eye so that you may see your picture first with the spiritual eye. Then bring to the light of day that which you have seen in the inner darkness so that it may react on others from the outside inwards.' Friedrich does actually seem to have created his pictures with his 'inner' eye, conceiving them in his mind before drawing them out on his canvas (illustration 5). But this does not mean that he was inattentive to nature. Almost every form in his paintings, down to the smallest leaf, is based upon something that he had studied. The job of the 'inner' eye was to combine these forms in new ways that brought out a deeper meaning.

Friedrich had originally trained as a topographical artist, producing views of his native Pomerania.

When he first came to Dresden, he made his living selling such works. Gradually, however, under the influence of the Dresden Romantics, he became more ambitious and began to design works with symbolic content. By 1808 this process was fully developed. This was the year in which he painted the *Cross in the Mountains* (illustration 6). The picture created a sensation when it was exhibited in the artist's studio. To conventional critics – notably a local writer called the Freiherr von Ramdohr – it seemed to break all the rules of painting. The first, and most glaring infringement is the use for which the work was intended. It was designed to be an altar-piece – for use in the private chapel of the castle of Tetschen in northern Bohemia. Normally an altar-piece would show religious figures, such as Christ, the Virgin Mary or some saints. But Friedrich has shown instead a landscape. The point that he was making was that he felt the contemplation of nature was as spiritual an experience as the contemplation of saints or stories from the Bible. 'The divine is everywhere' he once argued, 'even in a grain of sand.'

The picture is so dramatic in its effect that it might at first sight seem unnatural. However, in central Europe it is common to see crucifixes on the tops of mountains. The real drama of the picture comes not from its imagery, but from the way in which Friedrich has presented it. We are shown nothing but the tip of the mountain, and this is viewed in such a

8 (above) Schinkel: 'The Hall of Stars of the Queen of the Night'. Engraving after design for Mozart's 'Magic Flute'.
Schinkel's design perfectly complements the mysterious, masonic intentions of Mozart's opera. The magical effect is produced by the overwhelming symmetry of the scene. As one critic said: 'So much can be achieved by simple ingenuity'.

9 (left) Friedrich: 'Two Men Contemplating the Moon'. Oil.
This painting has political overtones. The two men wear 'Old German' costume – the dress associated with revolutionaries. The figures have been identified as Friedrich himself and one of his pupils.

way as to form a striking silhouette against the evening sky. Here again the conventions of picture making had been flouted. At that time landscapes were normally expected to have foreground, middle-ground and background. But Friedrich cuts all this away to arrive at a dramatic and compelling image.

Such original uses of scenery soon made Friedrich a notorious figure. A few years later, in 1810, he had a major success when he sent a pair of large landscapes to be shown at the academy exhibition in Berlin. One showed a monk wandering along a barren shore, the other a funeral taking place in a ruined abbey surrounded by barren oak trees, the whole scene lost in the dusk. Once more Friedrich achieved his effects by his striking use of silhouettes and lighting, making natural forces seem charged with heightened meaning.

These two pictures were brought by the Crown Prince of Prussia. Friedrich's success now seemed secure. However, the fascination with his striking, unusual style of painting was to some extent dependant upon the special circumstance of his times. A great surge of national feeling had been stimulated by the invasion of Germany by Napoleon in 1806. This invasion was eventually repulsed in 1814. In the intervening years there was a great taste for those works of art that appeared to have a natural flavour, and which kept alive the image of the German people as a vigorous spiritual force. Friedrich's images – with their emphasis on northern landscapes and mystical effects – seemed particularly relevant. He was, in fact, extremely patriotic. Like Runge – who designed an allegory on the *Fall of the Fatherland* – he painted works which had direct political associations. One depicted a French huntsman lost in a German forest of evergreens. It was shown in 1814 in an exhibition that celebrated the defeat of the French.

Friedrich's impact

It is hardly surprising that Friedrich's pictures should at this time have inspired other artists. In Berlin the great architect Karl Friedrich Schinkel (1781–1841) turned to landscape painting. This was largely because the privations of the Napoleonic Wars had brought about a cessation of most building projects in Prussia. Schinkel was deeply impressed by Friedrich's dramatic use of lighting. He used a similar type of effect in his *Gothic Cathedral by a River* (illustration 7). Painted in 1814, this picture also had political overtones. The splendid cathedral, soaring above a river, was seen as an image of national regeneration. This picture was a fantasy, but a few years later such a project was actually put into practice. Under the protection of the Prussian king, the medieval cathedral of Cologne was completed and became for many Germans a symbol of their nation's restoration.

Since 1806 Schinkel had also been working as a scene painter. At first he painted *dioramas* (illuminated scenery), but after 1815 he was also employed as a designer by the Berlin Royal Theatre. In this capacity he experimented with that inter-

10 (below) Friedrich: 'The Arctic Shipwreck'. Oil. *Here Friedrich depicts the classic Romantic theme of man at the mercy of the elements. Turner chose such subjects to highlight the human drama, but Friedrich concentrates on the inevitable conclusion, as the ship is crushed by great pyramids of ice.*

relationship of the arts that had so fascinated Runge and other romantic theoreticians. His interest in the association of pictorial scenery with music and poetry was most fully engaged in his designs for opera. For Mozart's *Magic Flute* he conceived a series of designs in 1815 that seemed a perfect accompaniment to the opera's mysterious intentions. The overwhelming symmetry of the *Hall of Stars of the Queen of the Night* (illustration **8**) is the most remarkable of these. As with his *Gothic Cathedral by a River,* these designs had a political meaning. The performance of *The Magic Flute* for which they were intended was a celebration of the restoration of peace. In this context Mozart's mystical fable became an affirmation of the Prussian state's triumph over the tribulations of the Napoleonic period.

After the Napoleonic Wars, Friedrich's art began to fall out of favour. His painting now came to be regarded as eccentric. Furthermore, his own political views isolated him. Friedrich was not only a nationalist. He was also a liberal, who wanted the overthrow of the feudal régimes of the German principalities. In the years following the defeat of Napoleon, most German governments became increasingly reactionary. Friedrich never took part in any overt protest against these. But his pictures often contain hints of his beliefs. His *Two Men Contemplating the Moon* (illustration **9**) shows two men in 'old German' costume, a style of dress that was associated with liberals and revolutionaries. The figures have been identified as Friedrich himself, and one of his pupils.

During these years Friedrich's art changed. He moved away from the depiction of monks, ruins and crosses, and painted instead contemporary scenes, such as the *Arctic Shipwreck* (illustration **10**). This is one of a number of shipwreck scenes that he painted in the 1820s. Like his contemporary, the English painter Turner, and other Romantic artists, Friedrich was fascinated with natural disasters for the way in which they pitted man against the elements. This picture, which shows a ship being slowly ground to pieces in an ice-bound sea, seems to suggest that the struggle is a futile one. But in the background is a calm blue sky and a burst of light – indications of the promise of eternity beyond this life.

The medieval revival

At the same time that Runge and Friedrich were developing a visionary form of landscape, other German artists were looking in a different direction, and modelling their art on that of the Middle Ages. They were inspired by Romantics like Friedrich Schlegel, who believed that the modern world had become unbearably pagan and materialistic. Such people looked to the Middle Ages as an age of humble faith, when spiritual values dominated society. For Germans there was an added attraction to this period. It had been a time when Germany had enjoyed political unity, under the Holy Roman Empire. This contrasted with the present age, when it was divided into a mass of small states.

In the early years of the 19th century, groups of artists imitating the styles of medieval art sprang up throughout Germany – particularly after 1806, when Napoleon's invasion gave a new spurt to nationalism.

11 (left) Overbeck: 'Franz Pforr'. Oil.
Overbeck and Pforr were the leaders of the 'Nazarenes', a brotherhood of artists who harked back to the Middle Ages.

12 (below) Schwind: 'The Symphony'. Oil.
Schwind's painting forms a direct link between music and the visual arts. Indeed, his gently flowing line has been compared with the lyrical effect of music. In this ambitious work, Schwind combines a number of scenes in a way that reflects the different themes in a piece of music. In the lower scene a concert is actually taking place, and Schubert can be spied in the left background.

The most influential group emerged in Vienna. This was the 'Brotherhood of St Luke', which was founded in 1808 by some students of the Vienna Academy. As can be seen from the portrait by one of the leaders, Friedrich Overbeck (1789–1869) of the other, Franz Pforr (1788–1812) (illustration 11), they took their medievalism very seriously indeed. They tried to use the simple forms and bright colours that they associated with medieval art. And they also affected a medieval lifestyle, growing their hair long, wearing flowing robes and living for a time in a quasi monastic community. In 1810 they moved to Rome to be closer to examples of medieval art and to the centre of Christianity. Here their long hair gained them the nickname 'Nazarenes' – that is, people who had a Christ-like appearance. As they grew more famous, their art became more pious and stilted. They never achieved their aim of restoring the values of medieval society, but they were to remain influential among religious painters for more than half a century.

It is hard to see many connections between this group and the principal developments in the music of the period. But the medieval revival did involve music in other ways. One was through the renewed interest in folk culture, which was seen as a living, vernacular, branch of medieval art. Indeed, collections of ballads, fairy tales and folk-songs were widespread at this time. The most famous product of this interest was the Grimm brothers' collection of Fairy Tales (1812–22). In music this interest led to the practice of including folk-tunes in pieces – something that Beethoven did at times. It also led to the development of *Lieder* – lyrical songs which drew upon the traditional themes and forms – a musical form perfected by Franz Schubert.

Moritz von Schwind (1804–71)

In painting, some artists also turned to folk art and legends for their inspiration. The most important of these was Moritz von Schwind (1804–71) who frequently illustrated fairy tales painting pictures with a strong lyrical mood. It has often been remarked that the flowing 'melodic' line evident in Schwind's designs has a musical character.

A Viennese by birth, he was a close friend of Schubert's. He was himself a highly gifted violinist and once remarked that one should have a 'mouthful of music' every day. He attempted to reproduce the effects of music in several of his pictures. One of his most ambitious works was entitled *The Symphony* (illustration 12), and brought together a group of scenes in a way that he felt mirrored the association of themes and motifs in a musical composition.

Interesting though such connections are, they do have their limitations. Schwind is always in danger of becoming the mere illustrator of musical effect. While his pictures have a lyrical charm that is reminiscent of Schubert, they hardly have the subtlety, profundity and emotional breadth of the works of that composer. They are, perhaps, a warning against using one art form too closely to imitate the qualities of another. Paradoxically, more telling parallels between art and music emerge when each is exploring its own properties. From this point of view Runge and Friedrich share more of the qualities of the German music of the early 19th century. For they were each concerned with radically rethinking the basis of their art – discovering new ways of using form, light and colour to express their dramatic and original visions.

'The Corsican ogre'

Few events have determined the course of world istory as much as the French Revolution and fewer still have thrown up such a monolithic figure as Napoleon – visionary, tactician and despot.

In the bloodbath years following the storming of the Bastille the French constitution was vandalized by successive, well-meaning, but quite unworkable, attempts at government. From 1789 to 1791 the deputies in the Constituent Assembly, as the new governing body was now called, set about the task of creating a new France. The most intractable problem concerned the fate of the Catholic Church and the massive debt inherited from the Bourbons. The immense landed wealth of the Church was seized and used, through the introduction of a new form of currency, the *assignat,* to pay off the debt. But there remained the problem of the relationship between the assembly and the king – and that of the relationship between the assembly and the popular movement.

In 1791 the king still had important powers – he could in fact veto legislation passed by the assembly – and power had not yet passed to the people. In that year, in a fit of panic, the royal family made an abortive attempt to escape from France and, in doing so, made a mockery of the 'constitutional monarchy'. And then a month later a demonstration of republicans was re-pressed with some bloodshed by the National Guard. It seemed that both the king and the majority of the poor were unsatisfied with the Revolution's reforms. The Constituent Assembly gave way in 1791 to a completely new body, the Legislative Assembly.

The new body was not averse to war. Its leaders favoured a revolutionary crusade to unite an increasingly divided nation. In April 1792 war was declared on Austria and Prussia – powers that threatened to overthrow the revolution.

Patriotic revolutionary forces were unleashed by the war and the Parisian crowd stormed the Tuileries palace where the king had been kept virtually a prisoner since 1791. The overcrowded prisons were invaded and over 1000 suspected traitors were killed – no government could now afford to ignore the potentially explosive force of the Parisian crowd. For the remainder of the Revolution events would be dictated largely by two factors – the quality of the harvest and success or failure on the field of battle.

The king was executed in January 1793 and by March – repelled by the new direction the revolution was taking – the region of the Vendée in western France exploded in a spontaneous outburst of hostility. The government (now the National Convention) was faced with defeat abroad and civil war at home. The Jacobins, dominated by Maximilien Robespierre, seized power, drove foreign armies from France, quashed the royalist threat in Vendée, and launched the revolution on its expansionist phase.

Though the economy was stabilized and the hungry were fed the Jacobin period was one of quickening fanaticism. Two thousand 'traitors' in and around Nantes were killed, 5000 'counter-revolutionaries' in Lyons were liquidated. The Reign of Terror had begun.

Many regions of France were teetering on anarchy in 1793, but Robespierre and his colleagues in the Committee of Public Safety gradually centralized power. Opposition was mercilessly crushed; one-time leading lights of the revolution were led to the guillotine – Danton and his followers and Robespierre and his. They became the last noble victims of the terror after a political coup by the so-called 'Thermidoreans' in July 1794.

The young Napoleon embodied the Romantic ideal of individual struggle and heroism. But after more than a decade of bloody campaigns his image changed to that of a ruthless despot.

With the end of Robespierre and the Terror, power shifted yet again and by 1795 the bourgeoisie had the whip hand rather than the Parisian crowd. With the threat of royalist terrorism mounting, the Constitution of 1795 vested power in a Directory of five, a compromise between a fragile democracy and total dictatorship. The Directory lurched from one crisis to the next. Governed by officials who were at best cynical, at worst corrupt, and overwhelmed with the problems of spectacular military expansion, in 1799 the Directory finally succumbed. A young Corsican general seized power and began to clear up the debris of a decade of revolution. Napoleon Bonaparte was at the centre of the stage.

The rise of Napoleon

Napoleon was, it has been argued, 'the most powerful genius who ever lived', scourge of kings and defender of the great ideals of the French Revolution; a statesman of principle and an administrator of unparalleled ability; a spectacular warrior, yes, but one driven time and again into battle by the enmity of the reactionary forces ranged against revolutionary France.

To those who feared and hated him he was the sleek-haired 'Corsican ogre', and a generation of English nursemaids would terrorize squealing children with the awful warning that if they did not stop crying 'Boney' would come and devour them. He was a ruthless tyrant, cold, manipulative and indifferent to the sufferings he inflicted on humanity.

Born on 15 August 1769 Bonaparte completed his schooling at the Ecole Militaire in Paris in 1785. He then embarked on what was to become the greatest military career in history.

Like his military tactics, Napoleon's career was marked by breathtaking speed and resolute doggedness. In 1791 he was promoted to lieutenant and the following year to captain. For Napoleon, 1793 was to

be a critical year: the Revolution was rapidly turni[ng] bloodier, Louis XVI and Marie Antoinette had be[en] executed, France had thrown down the gauntlet at t[he] feet of the world's powers while internally she w[as] torn by rebellion in several provinces.

The Revolutionary government recoiled in sho[ck] when Toulon, a significant naval base, defected fro[m] the Republic and admitted an Allied force und[er] Admiral Hood. All attempts to take the town had be[en] repulsed, until Napoleon, as fate would have it, to[ok] over from a wounded gunner. It was a propitio[us] moment; the young officer applied his vast energy a[nd] military inventiveness to the siege of Toulon. Und[er] his direction the town was reoccupied by Fren[ch] forces and as his reward Napoleon was ma[de] Brigadier-General. His age was just over 24.

Appointed to the army in Italy he was a decisi[ve] factor in the French victory at Loano in 1794. B[ut] there followed a greater opportunity which [he] grasped with characteristic speed. In October 17[95] the Paris mob rose against the Directory and it fell [to] Napoleon with his salvoes of cannon, his so-call[ed] 'whiff of grapeshot', to quell the rebellion. His succe[ss] won for him instant praise and, ten days lat[er] promotion to Commander of the Army of the Interio[r].

Whatever else Napoleon Bonaparte may have bee[n] he was first and foremost a soldier, and it was as [an] artillery officer in the armies of revolutionary Franc[e] that the young Corsican first distinguished himse[lf]. From 1792 onwards, France was constantly at war wi[th] various combinations of her continental neighbou[rs] aided and abetted by Britain – all of them apalled [by] what they saw happening in France and fearful of th[e] implications of such upheaval. Quite apart from th[e] understandable horror inspired by the thud of th[e] guillotine blade, such ringing phrases as 'the Rights [of] Man' and 'Liberté, Fraternité, Egalité', sent tremo[rs] through the aristocratic societies of the late 18th

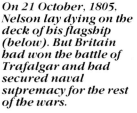

On 21 October, 1805, Nelson lay dying on the deck of his flagship (below). But Britain had won the battle of Trafalgar and had secured naval supremacy for the rest of the wars.

*apoleon fell
assionately in love
ith Josephine (right).
he was his mistress for
few months before
hey married in 1796.
uring Napoleon's
ng absences abroad,
osephine dabbled
reely in love affairs
nd the marriage
ooked ready to
ollapse. But finally it
as her failure to
roduce an heir that
ecided Napoleon to
ivorce her. In 1810 he
arried Marie-Louise,
aughter of the
ustrian Emperor.*

century which reverberated all through Europe.

Bonaparte rose at lightning pace through these campaigns, to take command of the Army of Italy (the French army designated for action in Italy) in 1796, at the age of 27. The campaign that followed made him a national hero: a *blitzkrieg* through northern Italy where he scored a dozen resounding victories in as many months. He was then given command of the Army of England, and promptly set about planning the downfall of France's most dangerous enemy – as she had been for the past hundred years. After careful examination of the possibilities Bonaparte concluded that a direct assault across the English Channel would fail, so he chose instead a most audacious indirect form of attack – through Egypt to India, which would both demoralize Imperial Britain and cripple a vital area of her commerce.

The French expeditionary force which set sail from Toulon in May 1798 met with initial success – first Malta, then Alexandria and the Nile delta falling before it. But a crushing defeat at the hands of Horatio Nelson in the Battle of the Nile of 1 August ruined the grand design, and Bonaparte eventually escaped back to France leaving his army behind.

The failure in Egypt did nothing to diminish his ambitions, nor indeed to harm his prospects – within a month he had conspired successfully to stage a bloodless *coup d'état,* from which he emerged as First Consul. He would go on to promote himself to First Consul for Life in 1802 and finally crown himself Emperor of France in 1804, but from this moment in November 1799 he was effectively master of France.

There was only the briefest of pauses while Napoleon consolidated his power and reorganized the military forces now at his sole command, and then in the spring of 1800 he struck at northern Italy again, where an Austrian army was beseiging Italy. Having made their way through the snow-covered St. Bernard

Wellington did far more than lend his name to a boot. He hounded Napoleon throughout the Iberian Peninsula and finally defeated him at Waterloo.

Napoleon achieved the pinnacle of his career and the height of his formidable arrogance on 2 December, 1804, when he declared himself Emperor. Although the Pope was brought to Paris for the ceremony Napoleon placed the crown on his own head.

Pass, the French fell upon and defeated the Austrians at Marengo on 14 June. A further shattering defeat at the hands of a French army in Germany later that same year knocked Austria right out of the war – leaving Britain and France glaring hatred at each other across the Channel but with neither able to do much about it. Fulminate as they might against the dreadful 'Boney', there was no way the British could challenge his supremacy on the Continent. Scheme as he did to bring down 'the nation of shopkeepers', the British Fleet still stood between Napoleon and complete victory. It was stalemate, and on 25 March 1802 the two nations signed a peace treaty at Amiens. The opening phase of the Napoleonic wars was over.

Invasion plans

There was never any realistic hope that the Peace of Amiens would last for long: it was no more than a temporary armed truce between irreconcilable enemies. In May 1803, after a mere 14-month respite, the war was resumed, and resumed in such a way as to give the British nation a terrible fright. With no one left on the Continent with the stomach to fight him, at least for the time being, Napoleon was free to concentrate the entire weight of his military machine on a cross-channel invasion. Over the next two years a huge army – the Grand Army – was assembled at the Channel ports, and some 200 flat-bottomed boats were built capable of transporting fully 200,000 battle-hardened soldiers to the south coast of England.

However, the prerequisite for invasion of England was, as always, control of the Channel. Napoleon's strategy was chess-like in its complexity, but basically it involved luring the British fleet into the Western Atlantic, so that a combined French and Spanish fleet could sweep unopposed up the Channel to Boulogne, there to rendezvous with the invasion flotilla. Britain's fate would be sealed.

What happened in fact was that the French fleet under Admiral Villeneuve was hounded back and forth across the Atlantic by Nelson, and finally driven to ta refuge in Cadiz. On 19 October 1805 Villeneuve ve tured forth to do battle – against his better judgeme but on the express order of an incensed Napoleo Two days later, on the 21st, his fleet was annihilated Cape Trafalgar in one of history's most celebrated nav engagements. The great invasion scare was lifte although an end to hostilities was as far away as ever

More French victories

Crushing victories over the Austrians at Ulm, and ov combined Austrian and Russian forces at Austerlitz 2 December 1805 made it plain enough once again tha on land, the French were still invincible. Prussia w rash enough to enter the fray belatedly the followi year, only to have her armies destroyed on 14 Octob at Jena and Auerstädt. And if there was still any dou as to who was master of Europe it was settled in t summer of 1807, at Friedland, where the Grand Arr inflicted 25,000 casualties on the Russians.

At this stage Napoleon the soldier gave way Napoleon the diplomat. In his celebrated meeting of July 1807 with Tsar Alexander I, on a raft anchored the Nieman river in northern Prussia, he succeeded prising Russia away from the alliance with Britain. the Treaty of Tilsit, Napoleon and Alexander effective divided the Continent into two great spheres influence, Russian in the east and French in the we This was probably the high point of Napoleon's fo tunes, and it freed him once again to direct his aw some energy and willpower to the destruction Britain.

Trafalgar had ended conclusively any dream naval supremacy and invasion. The only way bring Britain to her knees was by destroying h commerce, and the only way to destroy her commerc was to establish a 'fortress' Europe – a Europea continent from which British trade was total excluded. This in turn implied sealing off the enti coast of western Europe, Atlantic and Mediterranea

Mary Evans Picture Library

'Coronation of Napoleon' by Jacques-Louis David: Louvre/Scala

it was that Napoleon turned his gaze for the first
e on the Iberian peninsula, and in particular on
tugal, Britain's traditional ally. Given the unlimited
le of his ambitions, and the intransigence of Britain
he face of them, the logic of this step was probably
scapable. And yet it was here, at the height of his
cess, that Napoleon set off on the long road to
terloo.

t was easy enough to march through Spain and
upy Lisbon, towards the end of 1807, and to topple
Spanish crown the following year – where
oleon installed his brother Joseph as king. The
blem, and it was one he had not encountered before,
that the Spanish and Portuguese populations rose
arms against the French invader. Years of inter-
able, savage guerilla warfare lay ahead, and even
rse from the French standpoint the chaos enabled
tish forces to form a bridgehead on the Continent.
Arthur Wellesley, later Duke of Wellington,
umed command of the British army in Portugal in
9, and, while for several years the Peninsular War
ained a bloody sideshow to the greater theatres
war to the east, it was from there that Wellington
uld eventually return in triumph to London – by
y of Paris.

r with Russia

Napoleon's attempt to subjugate Spain and Portugal
s a mistake, his break with the Tsar and attempt
ually to conquer Russia was a calamity. The Treaty
Tilsit, on the face of it an admirable arrangement for
h sides, could not long be sustained. Aside from
r of provoking Napoleon's wrath, the Tsar had no
entive to stamp out trade with Britain, and he
an to turn a blind eye to his merchants' evasion of
regulation banning that trade – the so-called
ntinental System. Moreover, Russia had designs on
and and the Balkans, which Napoleon would not
erate. On both counts, therefore, the Tsar had to be
ught to heel, and in the spring of 1812 Napoleon

amassed a force of half a million men.

Contrary to his expectations, such a show of force
did not intimidate the Tsar, and towards the end of
June the Grand Army struck out for Moscow. Seventy-
five miles short of the goal, on 7 September 1812, one
of the goriest engagements of the entire Napoleonic
era was fought to a standstill – The Battle of Borodino.
Technically a French victory, in that the Russians
withdrew, leaving Moscow undefended and indeed
deserted, it was a victory that cost Napoleon as dear as
any defeat could have done. He held an empty Moscow,
but he had not destroyed the Russian army, and could
no longer escape the dreadful conclusion that he had
won nothing at all, and that he must retreat before the
onslaught of Russian winter. So began one of the most
ghastly episodes in the annals of warfare. Starving,
freezing, stumbling through blinding snow storms;

*Beethoven's 'Eroica'
symphony was almost
certainly inspired by the
ideal of Napoleon as
champion of freedom,
but the intended
dedication was
scrawled out (above).*

*After what was perhaps
the goriest battle of the
Napoleonic wars – the
indecisive battle of
Borodino, 1812,
Napoleon occupied a
near-deserted Moscow.
In the end he had no
option but to begin the
long retreat (below).*

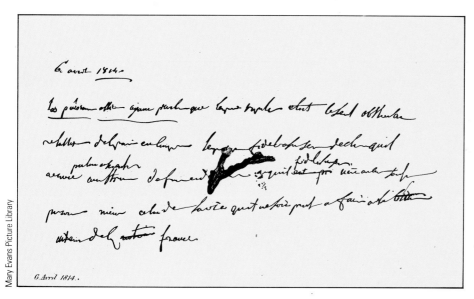

G. Avril 1814.

Napoleon's unconditional abdication of 6 April, 1814 (above). A month later, with a guard of 600 soldiers, he was on his way to the island of Elba and exile. But within a year he'd escaped and was back mustering another army.

harassed on all sides by Russian snipers and decimated by the icy torrents of the river Beresina, the tattered remnants of the Grand Army straggled back towards Poland. Of the 600,000-odd troops who entered Russia little more than 100,000 returned. It was to be a turning point in the Emperor's career.

The disastrous Russian campaign doomed Napoleon – and not least because it shattered the myth of invincibility that had so long surrounded him. Russia, Austria and Prussia were now all ranged against him in the east, while Wellington was advancing remorselessly from the south-west.

At the Battle of Leipzig in October 1813, what was left of the Grand Army was smashed beyond repair; Wellington crossed the Pyrenees in November; in December the Prussians advanced across the Rhine. Twist and turn Napoleon might, in a dazzling series of defensive manoeuvres, but the trap was sprung and there was no escape. On 31 March 1814 the victorious allies entered Paris; Napoleon was forced to abdicate – an unconditional surrender, in fact – and he was exiled with a retinue and pension to the Mediterranean island of Elba.

Waterloo

For the allies to leave Napoleon in relative comfort close to home, considering how much they had suffer at his hands, may strike modern observers as bei unduly generous to a vanquished foe. It certai proved dangerous. At the beginning of March 1815 staged a dramatic escape from Elba, rallying suppo on all sides from peasants and ex-soldiers as marched triumphantly north to Paris. So began t famous 'Hundred Days', the desperate last throw o man who could not countenance defeat and who cou still inspire fierce loyalty even in a palpably lost cau. Obviously the allies would not stand idly by, a Napoleon characteristically went straight over to t offensive, marching his Old Guard into Belgium confront the British and Prussian armies marshalli against him. On 16 June he defeated the Prussians Ligny, but two days later at Waterloo Wellingto army, reinforced at a critical moment by the Prussia brought this extraordinary chapter of European histo to a close. And this time the allies took no chanc They exiled their enemy thousands of miles away the south Atlantic island of St. Helena.

The Europe he left behind would never be the sar again, however keen the victorious powers might to reverse the currents set in train by the Fren Revolution and the massive upheavals caused by years of warfare. For however dreadful the carnage had wrought in pursuit of his military ends, Napole had in fact been responsible for implanting many the ideals of the Revolution as far and wide as I conquests had taken him. Or, looked at another w he had torn apart so much of the fabric of an old order that it was quite impossible ever to restore it.

The map of Europe itself had been irreversib changed. To take only one example, Germany in 18(had been a patchwork of 396 petty principalities a free cities, a hold-over from medieval times. Napole reduced it to 40, and this was an essential step the development of a modern Germany. Wherever t French armies passed, they left behind the Fren Civil Code – which embodied concepts like individu liberty and equality before the law. Reactionary forc might show little enthusiasm for such ideals, but th would prove remarkably difficult to stifle.

Finally defeated at Waterloo Napoleon sails (right) on the HMS Bellerophon for the distant island of St Helena from which there was to be no escape. He spent his last years dictating memoirs and contemplating what might have been. He died there on 5 May, 1821, aged 51.

IN THE BACKGROUND

The House of Hapsburg

From 1792 until his death in 1827, Beethoven made his home in Vienna, the capital of the large and somewhat unwieldy domains ruled by the Hapsburg family, which at that time and throughout Beethoven's life was headed by Francis II. Vienna, like the rest of the Hapsburg lands, suffered badly during the French Revolutionary and Napoleonic wars – during the 1809 bombardment, Beethoven had to shelter in a friend's cellar, protecting his failing hearing with pillows tied over his head. After the defeat of Napoleon, the Hapsburgs – though they lost the hereditary title of Holy Roman Emperor – consolidated their territories and, as Emperors of Austria, continued to control much of central Europe until the end of the Great War, when the subject peoples rose against Hapsburg rule, the empire was broken up and the map of Europe was once again redrawn.

'Happy Austria'

The Hapsburgs ruled a vast and sprawling empire, surviving wars, revolutions and intrigues through their cunning and resilience. For 600 years they influenced history – but finally it overtook them.

Of all the great royal families the Hapsburgs have been by far the most influential over the widest area for the longest time. For seven centuries, extending into our own, this remarkable family held unbroken sway over vast domains scattered around Europe and far beyond. It did this by a combination of luck, ability and above all sheer tenacity of purpose. Especially so when it came to the matter of the survival and aggrandizement of the House of Hapsburg, when necessary by war and at all times by shrewd dynastic alliance. This latter is neatly encapsulated in a line of Latin verse which translates: 'Others may conduct wars, while you,

happy Austria, conduct marriages.'

The Hapsburgs reached their zenith in the 16th century, when the Emperor Charles V could lay claim, by inheritance, to the most widely-distributed collection of lands the world had ever known. In 1530 Charles was crowned Holy Roman Emperor, a somewhat anachronistic title dating from Charlemagne which carried immense prestige and active power in the Hapsburg heartland of central Europe. This added to more than a score of titles he already possessed when he ascended the throne. Here is just a sample: he was King of Spain; King of the

The most powerful ruler since the Roman Emperors, Charles V established a firm foundation for the House of Hapsburg which would see it through to the 19th century. Depicted here a bunt in his honour, taking place before one of the many Hapsburg castles.

Charles V's coat of arms bearing the defiant Hapsburg insignia of the double-headed eagle declares him Holy Roman Emperor (left). He was crowned such by Pope Clement VII in 1530.

A magnificent Bruges tapestry (below) depicts Charles V, the newly proclaimed 'Lord of Africa', as a knight in shining armour.

Maria Theresa

Charles VI died unexpectedly in 1740, leaving no son, and bequeathing to his 25-year-old daughter Maria Theresa as hollow an inheritance as it is possible to imagine. She was heir to the Hapsburg lands in Austria and Germany, the Austrian Netherlands and some duchies in Italy, as well as to the crowns of Hungary and Bohemia. But the Hapsburg finances were in ruins – vast and mounting debts secured by mortgages on most of the Hapsburg domains. During his final years Charles had blundered into a ridiculously wasteful series of wars, against the Bourbons in France and Italy and then against the Turks of the Ottoman Empire. Consequently, Maria Theresa had no army worth maintaining and no money to raise one. Further, such central administration as there ever had been for this scattered empire had virtually ceased to function. Morale among those entrusted with governing had fallen to such a level that no one seems to have been able to give the young queen sensible advice, let alone reassurance. It is all too easy to believe the story that when one of her senior ministers spelt out the awful reality to her she maintained her composure, only to break down in tears a little later when she was alone with her lady-in-waiting.

omans; King of Sicily, Jerusalem and the Indies (that , the huge Spanish possessions in the Americas); he as Archduke of Austria; Duke of Burgundy and a host ? smaller principalities like Luxembourg, Syria and mburg; and for good measure, he was 'Lord of Asia d Africa'.

To put it mildly, this was an unwieldy onglomeration for even so able a monarch as Charles to administer effectively, and he sensibly hived off e traditional Austrian–Hapsburg lands to his brother rdinand, while keeping Spain and the rest for mself and his heirs. By the end of the 17th century, owever, the Hapsburg inheritance was beginning to ok a little frayed around the edges, as Bourbon ance forged ahead in terms of both wealth and ilitary might. Finally in 1700 disaster struck, when harles II of Spain died childless. Rival Hapsburg and ourbon claims to the vacant throne sparked off a ajor European and colonial war, the War of the panish Succession (1701–13), a war that ended conclusively in many respects but conclusively ough as far as the Spanish Succession was oncerned: the Hapsburgs lost it forever.

For the Emperor Charles VI in Vienna this was a ersonal disgrace and a savage blow to the Hapsburg ynasty. The Emperor took the disaster as a salutary arning. He too lacked an heir, and to avoid the readful prospect of the future dismemberment of the maining Hapsburg possessions he worked out a rmula which bore the enigmatic title, the 'Pragmatic anction'. By a decree signed in 1713 the Hapsburg nds were pronounced indivisible, and a clear line of accession was spelled out, starting with a son, should e have one, or a daughter, or failing that succession ould proceed in an orderly way throughout the mily. It was all very well to decree such a thing, owever, but making it stick would be another matter, nd it was with the Pragmatic Sanction that Hapsburg ustria entered a long and turbulent chapter that ould shake its foundations.

As if this catalogue of woes was not enough, Maria Theresa had the misfortune to have as a direct contemporary Frederick II, newly installed on the throne of Prussia. Among many other things, Frederick – Frederick the Great, as he would become – was a military genius and an unscrupulous opportunist, and he wasted no time in setting about seizing the Hapsburg lands he coveted. He immediately invaded the Bohemian province of Silesia, a populous, mineral-rich and fertile region which bordered on Prussia. This act of base treachery – Frederick had formally acknowledged the Pragmatic Sanction – was the opening shot in the War of Austrian Succession (1740–48). This war, too, would at one time or another embroil most of the European powers and spread as far afield as Canada and India, but for Maria Theresa it was no less than a desperate struggle for Hapsburg survival.

Austria emerged from the war bruised and battered, with Silesia lost forever to Frederick's Prussia and bits of her Italian possessions snapped up by Bourbon Spain. But against all the odds she did survive, and Maria Theresa's claim to her throne was put beyond challenge. In the midst of the war, in fact, after the French and Bavarians had been driven out of Prague, she arrived there triumphantly to be crowned Queen of Bohemia. And in 1745 she secured for her husband Francis the imperial crown of the Holy Roman Empire.

The imperial crown of the Holy Roman Empire (right) was made for Otto I in the 10th century. It symbolized the Emperor's role as a servant of Christ and the Empire's dominion of the world.

The arch enemy of Maria Theresa and the greatest threat to her territorial rights was Frederick the Great of Prussia (below). A brilliant military thinker, he described Maria Theresa as 'the wisest of all my enemies'.

Österreichische Nationalbibliothek

Emperor Charles VI (above) dressed in the grand fineries of the Spanish court. The loss of the Spanish crown irked him throughout his reign: it was a disgrace to him personally and to the Hapsburg family it was a calamity.

In the person of Maria Theresa, the Hapsburgs had their greatest stroke of good fortune. In the course of the war she had demonstrated the highest courage and fortitude in adversity, as she would do repeatedly in the course of her long reign. She combined bravery with generally wise political instincts, and a shrewd understanding of the realities of power. She was fundamentally decent, against a current of all-pervasive cynicism, and yet she would earn from her arch-foe Frederick the Great, the greatest cynic of all, the description of 'the wisest of all my enemies'.

Rebuilding the Empire

Now, at the age of 31 and having borne five of her eventual 16 children, Maria Theresa took stock of the situation following the Treaty of Aix-la-Chapelle in 1748. The steadily shrinking Hapsburg empire had escaped wholesale dismemberment by the skin of its teeth. It had long been in decline and would most certainly perish sooner rather than later unless radically overhauled. Characteristically, the Empress set about this task undaunted by the difficulties involved and unmoved by the opposition which reform was bound to attract. The aim was to reinvigorate the economy and increase the Hapsburg revenue, and on the basis of a well-filled treasury build and train a large army that could hold its own with any on the Continent, in particular against Frederick's crack Prussian blues.

To accomplish this scheme required a host of reforms ranging across the entire spectrum of Austrian society. Pivotal to it all was the establishment of a centralized bureaucracy which could impose the imperial will and vision on the Hapsburg domains. In close alliance with her astute Chancellor, Count Haugwitz, Maria Theresa began to steer Austria away from the medieval, feudal past into the mainstream of modern Europe. Enlightened measures were taken to promote both military and civil education, to encourage commerce, industry and agriculture, and to provide a sensible system of justice. Breaking down feudalism meant lightening the burden of the

The imperial crown of Rudolph II (left) (who was made Emperor in 1576) also appears in the painting of Charles VI (below, far left). Rudolph's reign was a near disaster for the Hapsburgs and paved the way to the ruinous Thirty Years' War.

Empress Maria Theresa in middle age, painted on the terrace of the Schönbrunn palace with her husband Francis and 13 of her 16 children. Joseph, heir to her throne, stands in the centre of the star pattern (below).

peasantry, who still existed in a state of serfdom, and curbing the inordinate power of the great landed magnates, who by long tradition treated their vast estates as more or less independent kingdoms, untaxed, unfettered and unchallenged.

In her approach to foreign affairs, too, Maria Theresa broke with tradition. Guided by a diplomat of masterful skills, Wenzel Anton von Kaunitz, she came to see that the Prussian threat could not be removed (or Silesia regained) unless Austria managed to ally herself with France. In other words, Kaunitz intended to turn inside out the usual network of alliances which seemed always to leave Austria at a disadvantage. This was an audacious goal, considering that no one except the Hapsburgs cared about preserving, let alone enhancing, the Hapsburg fortunes. Yet by diplomatic sleight of hand Kaunitz achieved his aim, and when the next conflagration broke out it found Austria, with France and Russia, ranged against Prussia and Great Britain. The Seven Year's War (1756–63) was the major showdown between Britain and France in their bitter struggle for colonial empire and the command of the seas. For Austria it proved the final attempt to wrest back Silesia from Prussia. Yet, though thwarted in this cause which had become a Hapsburg obsession, the Austria of Maria Theresa emerged from the Seven Years' War not only intact, but finally back on the world stage as a respected power. The Empress

Sometimes referred to as the 'peasants' Emperor', Joseph II is depicted here guiding a plough. He was one of the 18th century's most enlightened despots: in 1781 he abolished serfdom and, although a devout Catholic, dissolved the monasteries and tolerated Protestants in an unprecedented manner for a Hapsburg.

Joseph II (far right) with his brother Leopold in 1769. Joseph had been Emperor and co-Regent with his mother Maria Theresa for four years.

Viennese promenade before the magnificent Hofburg palace (below) which was the main residence of the Hapsburgs. Originally built as a medieval fortress, it was added to by each succeeding Hapsburg. By the 19th century it comprised a riding school, a national library and government buildings.

could return to the weighty matters of internal reform in comparative safety.

She might have been forgiven for thinking that now, after many arduous years, she could live out the rest of her reign in comparative tranquillity. However, her fate was to be different. In 1765 her husband and confidant the Emperor Francis, an amiable if unfaithful man to whom she was devoted, died. Their eldest son ascended the imperial throne as Joseph II, and for the remaining 15 years of her life ruled as co-regent with his mother. It proved to be an uneasy alliance in the years that lay ahead.

Joseph II

Joseph II was a remarkable man, some would say the most 'enlightened' of all the 'enlightened despots' thrown up by the 18th century. He was certainly the most radical, and it may not be going too far to suggest that he was a thorough-going revolutionary – although, given his position, he viewed revolution as something to be imposed from the top downwards. By temperament he was the complete autocrat, with the dictatorial cast of mind that comes with utter certainty.

Where his mother cajoled, he compelled; where she showed willingness to compromise, he showed determination to prevail. In many ways the antithesis of Maria Theresa, then, and hardly a lovable man. Yet his iron will, in harness with his mother's humane worldliness, made for a formidable combination as they pushed ahead with the task of modernizing their empire.

For the most part, Joseph's aims, if not his methods, were the same as his mother's: administrative reform to weld the empire into a cohesive whole; the

regeneration of all aspects of commercial life and agriculture to increase wealth and raise revenue; and, much more pronounced in Joseph's case, a consistent drive to alleviate the misery of the poorest members of society. When Maria Theresa died in 1780, Joseph was at last free to push these policies and all his other radical ideas to their logical conclusion. He did so with single-mindedness and utter consistency, as might be expected from one who explained the proper approach to ruling as follows:

Great things have to be accomplished at one stroke. All changes arouse controversy sooner or later. The best way of going about it is to inform the public of one's intention at once, and, after having made one's decision, to listen to no contrary opinion, and resolutely to carry it out.

In 1781 he abolished serfdom outright, which meant that millions of peasants throughout the Empire gained freedom of movement, and freedom to pursue any chosen occupation. This decisive step was made doubly important by the terms of their emancipation. Elsewhere in Europe at the time, where serfdom was being abolished, it was common practice to part the serf from his land while unburdening him from his obligations to his landlord, thereby creating a huge class of landless labourers. Joseph, by contrast, guaranteed hereditary tenure of land to the freed serfs. Of course this infuriated the landlords, but Joseph seemed ever to take pleasure in infuriating the most powerful of his subjects. In fact he went so far as to say that the entire class system should be abolished.

His approach to religious affairs and in particular to the power of the Church was equally radical. He was

himself a devout Catholic, but that did not deter him from dissolving monasteries, removing Church control of press censorship, reforming the education of the clergy and granting a large measure of toleration to other sects and religions. The Pope made a special journey to Vienna to stem this tidal wave of reform, but not even His Holiness could prevail over Joseph.

These examples give only a hint of the zeal with which Joseph attacked the problem of governing his Empire, and, by implication, the enormous opposition his steam-roller tactics attracted. And they ignore the major failures of his final years, in particular his failure either to impose his will on his enemies in Hungary and the Netherlands or to make his peace with them. Both were in open revolt when he died in 1790. As uncompromising with himself as he was in every other way, he left behind the stony epitaph: 'Here lies Joseph II, who failed in all his enterprises'. It was too harsh a judgement.

Francis II

Joseph was succeeded by his younger brother Leopold, but at this stage in the Hapsburg saga it is the fortunes of their sister, Marie Antoinette, wife of Louis XVI and Queen of France, that command attention. The French Revolution was underway and gathering momentum, and in its wake would come a quarter of a century of mass turmoil and warfare that would shake European society from top to bottom. Yet again it would be the Hapsburg talent for sheer survival that would be put to the test. Leopold's son, who succeeded him as Francis II in 1792, was a born survivor, as remarkable for his equanimity and stolid patience as his mercurial uncle had been for his restless vigour. His most useful quality – it was priceless under the

circumstances – was the ability to bend before the winds without falling into despair, to endure humiliation when it was visited upon him in the unshakable belief that sooner or later his and Austria's day would come.

It was a long time coming. First the Netherlands fell to the armies of Revolutionary France in 1794. Then two years later the young Napoleon Bonaparte stripped the Italian cities of Milan and Mantua away from the Hapsburg Empire. That was just the beginning. The Napoleonic Wars were one long nightmare for Austria, as for others, but it was she who for the most part bore the brunt of the land fighting and she who came closest to permanent eclipse among the great powers. Napoleon crushed the Austrian armies at Austerlitz in 1805, and the following year imposed a peace treaty of unmitigated harshness which reduced Hapsburg authority and prestige to near impotence. He even stripped Francis of his greatest title, Holy Roman Emperor, by the simple expedient of abolishing the Holy Roman Empire. Francis, however, with customary prudence, had seen the way that particular wind was blowing, and had already provided himself with the brand new title Emperor of Austria.

With warfare going so disastrously wrong, Francis resorted to the other Hapsburg ploy, marriage. In 1810 he married his daughter Marie Louise to Napoleon, gaining thereby not so much an ally as a desperately needed respite from war. Three years later the tide was finally turning against his son-in-law, and Francis willingly joined the Grand Alliance with Britain, Russia and Prussia.

The Congress of Vienna

Hapsburg Austria not only survived this great upheaval, she now found herself at the centre of attention in a manner that would have seemed inconceivable only a short time before. Vienna was chosen to host the most magnificent assemblage of royal and political power ever witnessed in Europe. In September 1814 delegations poured in from all the victorious allies and from defeated France; their self-appointed task no less than that of putting the pieces of

99

*November 1805
Napoleon's Grand Army
entered Vienna (left)
after the crushing
Austrian defeat at
Austerlitz.

Using the time-honoured
political ploy of
marriage rather than
war, Francis II achieved
a clever coup in
marrying his daughter
Marie Louise to
Napoleon in 1810 (below
).

A years after its first
occupation by Napoleon,
Vienna played host to the
dignitaries of Europe
during the interminable
Congress of Vienna. In
this caricature (right)
are shown Tsar
Alexander I, Francis II
and Frederick William
of Prussia. Napoleon
looks on from his distant
Elbe.*

Bildarchiv Preussischer Kulturbesitz

fractured Europe back together again, and doing so in a way that would ensure peace for the forseeable future. Austria's brilliant foreign minister, Clemens von Metternich, worked night and day to engineer a peace settlement that would not only restore the Hapsburg possessions, but restore them within an overall settlement that would stand future strains. Peace and prosperity, but above all stability were the goals. For months the negotiations went on, against the glittering backdrop of European high society at play. The setting was sumptuous but the back-biting and the bickering were constant. While it continued Napoleon escaped from Elba and began his march on Paris. The final settlement was not thrashed out until nine days before Waterloo.

The Congress was a personal triumph for Metternich and a victory for the principles of monarchy and conservatism – the radical roots of the revolution and the real cry for liberty in its broadest sense had been buried. A return to pre-revolution conditions had been achieved – but only on paper. Metternich was a visionary; he saw Europe as an organic unity and wanted all its individual parts to prosper, especially his part – the Hapsburg Empire. But Metternich had reckoned without the tide of nationalism that was rising all over Europe.

Francis just wanted things to carry on much as before, to buy survival on the most economical terms. Out of the Congress he had lost the Netherlands, but he had gained a slice of Poland, a morsel of Bavaria and scattered pieces of Italy., He was well satisfied.

Growing unrest

After the Congress of Vienna Austrians busied themselves with economic expansion. Steam engines, power looms and other tools of industrial revolution were imported, factories set up, markets established. The growth impulse turned attention away from the

Francis II wearing the order of jewels of Emperor of Austria (left), a title he conferred upon himself when he shrewdly anticipated the end of the Holy Roman Empire. He was succeeded by Ferdinand (below) who was not mentally equipped to rule.

Kunsthistorisches Museum, Vienna/Bridgeman Art Library

Scala

iron hand of repression that imposed censorship, encouraged political informers and tried to smother creativity and free speech. Perfectly reasonable demands for social justice from the intelligentsia were interpreted by the establishment as the grumblings of insurrection and they over-reacted with ferocity.

When Francis died in 1835 he left the throne to his son Ferdinand who was weak in body and mind. But this slow-witted Hapsburg was loved by all his subjects for his almost saintly innocence and Metternich relished his accession as a chance to work the strings of a puppet emperor. Ferdinand had not reigned long before the revolutionary murmurs in Europe had become a loud howl of protest that threatened the very existence of the Hapsburg line.

The name of Napoleon was again the rallying cry in Paris, when in February 1848 Louis-Philippe was driven from his throne and a new republic declared. This time it was the nephew of Bonaparte, Napoleon III, who seized power. After years of repression and with demands for a constitution ignored, Austria was tinder dry for revolution. The Paris revolt was spark enough.

It was not just a handful of radicals who were responsible. The new class of industrial workers, now unemployed and disenchanted, also had heart-felt grievances to air. And in Italy, Hungary, Czechoslovakia and Germany, where the Hapsburg eagles still hovered, there was a growing clamour for dismantling the Austrian multi-national state and for recognizing the rights of independent nations.

On 13 March 1848 revolt at last broke out in Vienna It started quietly with university students voicing their demands for a measure of constitutional rights free speech and a liberal parliament. At the same time demonstrations took place in Prague, Milan, Venice Cracow, and Budapest. The crowds levelled their anger at the State Council on which Metternich served and in retaliation the State Council ordered that the troops level their rifles and fire volleys into the crowds. Instead of seizing the chance to unify the Empire the State Council short-sightedly risked losing it entirely.

Between March and December things went from bad to worse. Metternich fled to England and Ferdinand was smuggled from city to city while the Empire somehow staggered along. Ferdinand lacked the brains to cope with the throne and the natural heir Archduke Charles, lacked the temperament. It fell to his wife, Sophie of Bavaria to show the way and she with the support of the generals, chose her son Francis Joseph, to wear the Hapsburg crown. It was a reign that would end with the First World War and bring to a close 600 years of Hapsburg rule.

The Hapsburgs badly mishandled what began as student demonstrations in 1848. These rapidly escalated into violent revolutions and spread to other Hapsburg domains including Milan (below). It marked the end of many chapters of history for the Hapsburgs and the beginning of their last.

IN THE BACKGROUND

Medical progress in the 19th century

Although we may not look forward to or particularly enjoy a stay in hospital, we do expect to be treated by doctors who can use a variety of equipment – from the simple stethoscope to a sophisticated scanner – accurately to determine our illness; who will perform any surgery under sterile conditions to reduce the risk of infection; and who will use anaesthetics to prevent our feeling pain. This was not true for Beethoven and his contemporaries; indeed in his Heiligenstadt Testament, he complains of being 'aggravated and cheated by quacks'. In short, medical treatment was crude, ineffective and often hideously painful. Scientific developments in the 19th century transformed medicine into the science we know today, though sadly many people still find, like Beethoven, that there is no cure for their progressive deafness.

'The age of miracles'

In 1800 medicine was still in the dark ages –
disease and ignorance were rife. But a series of
scientific breakthroughs was soon to bring new
understanding of illness and its treatment.

A 17th-century doctor examines an anxious
patient's urine (above). This was one of the few
diagnostic techniques available in the days before
stethoscopes and thermometers.

The large towns and cities of the early 19th century
were disease-ridden and filthy places. Flea-infested
dogs roamed the streets and the drains were full of
rats. Most of the houses were damp and overcrowded,
and lacked both running water and effective
sanitation. In these circumstances outbreaks of
water-borne infectious diseases such as cholera and
typhoid were both frequent and devastating, and the
general lack of a good diet provided little protection
from the childhood diseases of diphtheria, scarlet
fever or measles.

At that time, expectation of life was no more than
40 years, and five out of every ten babies died. During
the first decades of the 19th century medicine could
offer little to the victims of infection, and many of the
Romantic composers, including Chopin and Schubert,
succumbed. It has been suggested that Beethoven's
deafness may have been due to an attack of meningitis in his youth. The composer did speak of a
'terrible typhoid' he had once suffered; at that time
this was almost a catch-all term for all fevers in which
the mind became clouded, including meningitis.

At the beginning of the 19th century ill-health was still thought to be caused by an excess of blood. Accordingly, sick and healthy people alike put their trust in the alleged benefits of regular bleedings. Here, one man (far left) is having leeches applied to his body and the other man (left) has had a vein cut by a doctor who is collecting his blood. Both these procedures were ways of drawing or letting blood.

The state of medicine

At the beginning of the century medical treatment was much as it had been for hundreds of years – crude and ineffective. The most common type of treatment was bleeding, which involved cutting a small vein with a knife or applying a jar full of leeches to the body. Both procedures had the same end: blood, an excess of which was thought to be the cause of disease, was drawn or 'let'. This drastic treatment, and that of 'purging' the body with a range of toxic solutions such as 'lead acetate and opium' or 'calomel opium and strychnine' (a deadly yet tranquillizing mix), was taught in all the European medical schools. When Mozart was on his death-bed suffering from rheumatic fever, the famous physician of the day who was treating him, Dr Sallaba, recommended that he should be bled. Many of Sallaba's patients were bled for hours, several times a day and this as much as anything decided Mozart's fate.

It was almost as bad to be given a doctor's prescription. The famous London surgeon, Robert Liston, described one patient suffering from venereal disease whose doctor had treated him with six courses of mercury (then a standard treatment for the affliction). The man's condition steadily grew worse. His mouth filled up with abscesses and ulcers as a result of the mercury, and because of the stench Liston was unable 'to come within an arm's length of him'.

In the 1830s very few doctors would even do so much as examine a patient. Diagnosis was usually based upon the patient's answers to questions about past illness and present appetite. The pulse was sometimes felt and the doctor also looked at the eyes and the tongue. Seldom, though, did he look for any obvious swelling or any other localized symptom of disease. The usual outcome was a 'purge' or a 'bleed', or some noxious concoction devised from the doctor's handbook of regular remedies.

The tools of the trade

In truth, doctors simply did not know enough about medicine. Although there is no doubt that many medical men made the most of their experience to benefit their patients, they could do little without the elementary tools that enabled them to carry out an objective physical examination. In 1800 there were

A country quack in his busy 'clinic'. The attentions of qualified doctors remained a luxury for most people in the 19th century but the cheaper quack's intimate knowledge of the community he served often compensated for his lack of formal medical training.

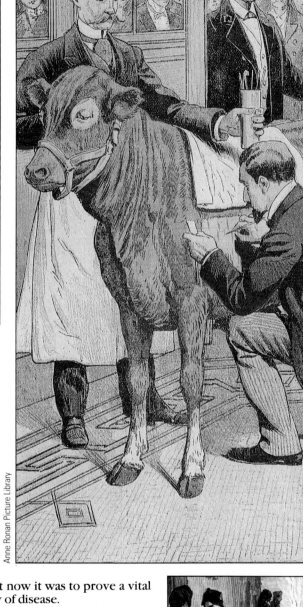

no X-rays, body-scanners, pathological tests or even simple stethoscopes. Medical diagnosis was based on the doctor's eyes and ears, and the will to use them.

The stethoscope was the first piece of diagnostic equipment to be developed. It was invented in 1816 by the French physician, René Laennec. His simple three-piece wooden tube was based upon the principle of percusson described 50 years earlier by an Austrian doctor called Leopold Auenbrugger. As a helper in his father's inn, Auenbrugger learned that wine barrels gave off different sounds when they were tapped, depending on how much liquid they contained. He later discovered that sounds could be heard when a patient's chest was tapped. These sounds, suggested Auenbrugger, depended upon the condition of the body's internal organs and, with Laennec's wooden stethoscope, they could now be amplified.

Later it was discovered that twin rubber tubes and earpieces running from a single tube, ending in the chestpiece, carried the sounds just as effectively as a single tube, and were much easier to use. This, essentially, is the form of stethoscope used by doctors today. Laennec's invention was slow to catch on, however, and in Britain doctors generally failed to learn how to use it properly. Much the same happened with early thermometers, which in the 1800s were as large as furled umbrellas and took about 20 minutes to register a temperature.

Until the 19th century, because of age-old scruples and religious restraints, the study of the human anatomy was largely based on the availability of dead criminals' bodies, or those supplied for payment by illegal 'body-snatchers'. But after 1800 more dead bodies could be openly and legally studied in the post mortem room. This gave the study of pathology (the scientific study of disease) an enormous boost, and encouraged physicians to look more closely at the bodies of living patients for signs of disease. Through pathology, the microscope suddenly came into its own and its design rapidly improved. The device had been in use for purely scientific purposes

Edward Jenner (above). His vaccine against smallpox worked on the principle that a dose of cowpox protected humans against the more lethal smallpox. One inoculation from animal to person was usually performed and from that person a human arm-to-arm 'chain' was set up. But the cow-to-arm inoculation method – here being done in Paris (right) – was often more hygienic.

for almost 200 years, but now it was to prove a vital aid for the detailed study of disease.

The agony of surgery

Until 1846, when anaesthesia was developed, surgery remained an appallingly painful experience. Operations generally took place in hospitals, although in rare cases, for rich clients, surgeons would operate in a private home. Most patients faced the knife in a grimy, ill-lit hospital operating theatre. There were no masks, gloves or sterilizing equipment. The surgeon himself might wear a suit, not a white coat, although many liked to work in a favourite frock coat and apron, which over the years would become encrusted with the blood and pus of the unfortunate patients.

For the patients an operation was unmitigated torture. Dragged unwillingly or carried from the ward to the operating room by burly attendants, the patient was seated on the table, or strapped down if necessary. The first cut with the scalpel was usually accompanied by loud shrieks of pain, ebbing away to convulsive sobs and cries as the terrible ordeal continued. Finally, exhausted by the pain of inflicted

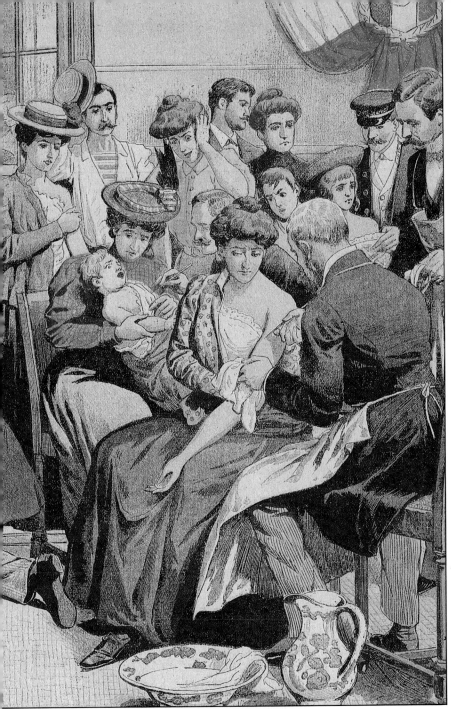

violence, the patient was carried back to the ward, usually to die of an infection.

Many of the medical students who watched such ordeals were put off medicine for life. When Charles Darwin was a medical student in Edinburgh in 1828 he witnessed such gruesome scenes. 'I saw two operations, one on a child, but I rushed away before they were completed. Nor did I ever attend again . . . the two cases fairly haunted me for many a long year.' James Simpson, the man who stumbled across the anaesthetic properties of chloroform in 1847, also shared Darwin's revulsion. He described how, as a student, he went on one occasion to see Robert Liston carry out an operation for amputation of the breast. Liston's technique 'was to lift up the soft tissues by an instrument resembling a bill hook, enabling the surgeon to sweep round the mass with his knife, in two clean cuts'. As the operation began, Simpson fled. He pushed his way through the crowds of young men and hurried out of the hospital and on up the hill to Parliament Square. He burst into the first imposing building he saw and demanded work as a clerk. Fortunately for all of us, he changed his mind on the following day.

Amputation was the commonest operation at this time because it was relatively simple and quick to perform. Surgeons would rarely cut into the abdomen or chest because of the risk of infection. Even so, some surgeons were bolder than others. In 1809 an American doctor called Ephraim McDowell, who had studied in Edinburgh, performed a successful ovariotomy (the removal of a cyst on the ovary). He had been called to see a patient in order to deliver 'twins', but he soon found that the woman had a large ovarian tumour, not twins. To wait meant certain death; to operate, according to the best medical opinion in Europe, also meant certain death through peritonitis. Nevertheless, McDowell offered to operate and his patient, a Mrs Crawford, consented. McDowell waited until Christmas Day to be sure of heavenly guidance and, miraculously, the 30-minute operation was a success. Mrs Crawford sang hymns while he removed her tumour and an anxious crowd from her village waited outside the operating room. Twenty-five days later Mrs Crawford – who must have been a very brave and robust woman – was fully

Fires of tar and sulphur are burned (far left) in an effort to disinfect the streets of Granada in Spain during the cholera outbreak of 1887. At the height of this epidemic people were dying at the rate of 500 a day. Before the connection between cholera and dirty water was made, the most bizarre precautions were taken – as this curious and ineffective 'anti-cholera' outfit of 1820 (left) demonstrates.

Bildarchiv Preussischer Kulturbesitz

The old operating theatre (right) at St Thomas's Hospital in London was used for 40 years after 1821. The primitive state of surgery then is evident from the bare, wooden operating table, the box of sawdust beside it (for collecting blood) and the stained surgeon's apron hanging on the back wall.

A cartoon of 1830 (below) features laughing gas 'frolics'. In time ether, and then chloroform, acquired a more serious use as an anaesthetic.

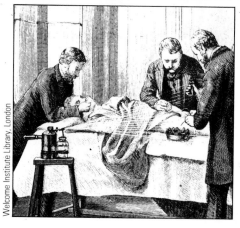

recovered and she lived to be a lively 78-year-old.

McDowell's fame spread across the Atlantic when more of his ovariotomy patients survived. His success was considered phenomenal because the death rate from such operations was usually well above 50 per cent. But, as with all other surgery, patients submitted to the knife because there was no other choice.

Pain put to sleep

With the advances in anatomy in the early 19th century surgery did reach a higher level of proficiency. But until the discovery of anaesthesia in 1846 even the most enterprising surgeons like McDowell came up against the barrier of pain. The mood-changing and pain-relieving powers of chemicals such as nitrous oxide had been known about long before 1846. Purely for entertainment, itinerant showmen enjoyed great success in staging demonstrations of the effects of 'laughing gas' (nitrous oxide), and medical students often amused themselves with ether 'frolics'. There had also been a great deal of interest in the strange phenomenon of suspended animation. Napoleon's chief surgeon, Baron Larrey, had written of an incident where several soldiers had become asphyxiated while sleeping in a badly ventilated room. Five of them were taken to hospital in a state of suspended animation, where three of them died. But the other two recovered completely.

Dentists were at the forefront of efforts to under-

stand the implications of such phenomena in order to produce a workable anaesthetic. In 1846 an American dentist called William Morton used ether to free one of his patients painlessly of an abscessed tooth. He was quick to publicize this feat and a few weeks later, at the Massachusetts General Hospital in Boston, Morton was given a chance to demonstrate his anaesthetic publicly. He duly administered ether and a surgeon, John Warren, was able to cut away a tumour from the neck of a young man, without the patient feeling the slightest pain.

At first Morton attempted to patent, and therefore profit from, his discovery by colouring the ether with chemicals and re-naming it 'Letheon'. But the nature of this substance became widely known within a short space of time and he soon dropped the idea. Morton failed to make his fortune through anaesthesia, but the impact of his sensational success at the Massachusetts General Hospital was immediate and world-wide. News of it reached Britain by ship, aboard the Cunard paddle steamer *Acadia,* which arrived in Liverpool from Boston in December 1846. Within days of the *Acadia's* arrival surgeons in Scotland and London had tried out what became known as the 'Yankee dodge'.

The ravages of infection

Ether, however, was both unpleasant for the patient and highly inflammable, and was quickly replaced by chloroform after James Simpson had discovered its anaesthetic properties. Chloroform, though, was also

Louis Pasteur (1822–95) in his laboratory (left). A giant in the history of medicine, his discovery of the germ theory led, among other advances, to Lister's antiseptic spray (below left).

Anaesthesia produced dramatic improvements in surgery by freeing patients from pain and allowing surgeons more precious time. But despite the sterilized instruments and uniformed nurses in this operation scene of the 1890s (below), Dr Péan and his team are still in street clothes.

dangerous to use, particularly during the early stages of light anaesthesia when it could interfere with the action of the heart. (We now know that it damages the liver as well.) But even so it had widespread use as a general anaesthetic for many years and was still in use well into the 20th century. Notwithstanding a persistent belief that pain in childbirth was God-ordained and therefore right, chloroform became particularly popular as a pain-reliever during labour. Queen Victoria herself was given the drug at the births of her two youngest children, Prince Leopold and Princess Beatrice. There was much resistance to this from conservative doctors, who were reluctant to see any risky new techniques tried on the monarch, but the Queen insisted: 'We are having this baby, and We are having chloroform.'

But even with anaesthetics, surgery had one further obstacle to overcome – infection. Very often a patient would survive the ordeal of the operating room only to die of a wound infection a few days later. Infection, or 'hospital disease', also claimed the lives of many women during or after childbirth. In

Vienna, for example, women would plead not to be admitted to the overcrowded delivery wards where, during ten days in May 1856, 31 out of 32 women died of puerperal fever following labour.

Florence Nightingale

Even the best hospitals at this time were dark, overcrowded and insanitary. It was not uncommon to see in the same ward cases of typhoid fever, pneumonia, dysentery and rickets, nor was it uncommon to see two patients in the same bed. This meant that many patients who entered with one complaint very quickly developed another, often with fatal consequences. Catholic countries to some extent enjoyed the relatively dedicated attention of nursing nuns, but nurses in Britain knew nothing of hygiene or cleanliness, being usually untrained women who were literally taken off the streets. The modern concept of the professional nurse had yet to evolve, and when it did it was largely due to the remarkable career of Florence Nightingale.

In 1853 an extremely able young woman from a

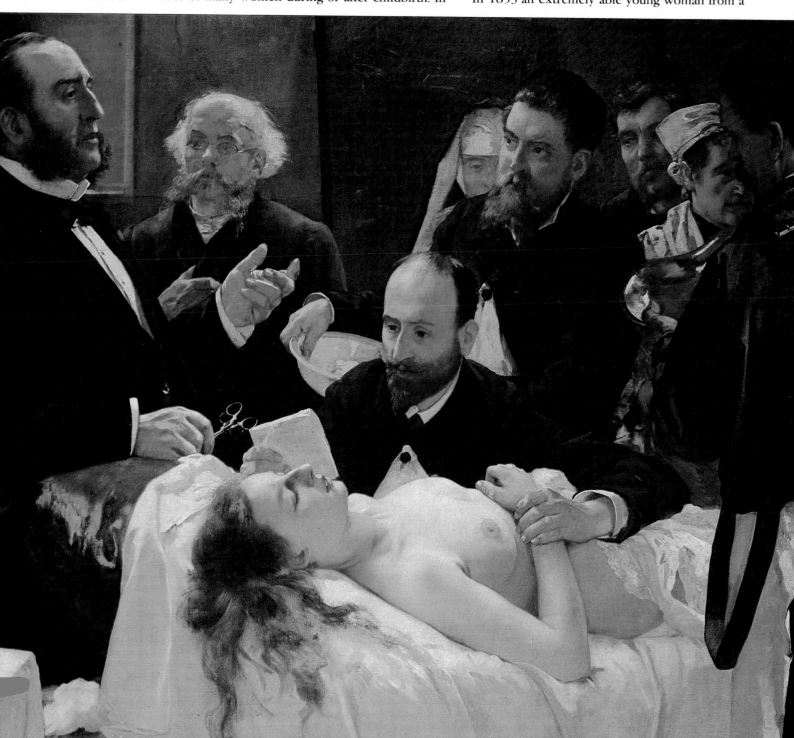

Florence Nightingale (above) did more than any other individual to change the dire conditions in Britain's hospitals and (as her influence grew) in the hospitals of many other countries. Central to her achievement was the raising of the status and quality of nurses by providing proper training.

wealthy background, who had become bored by the upper-class social round, undertook the management of a nursing home for 'Sick Gentlewomen in Distressed Circumstances' financed by charitable ladies. Having embarked on her career, Florence Nightingale (1820–1910) then took charge of the military hospital at Scutari during the Crimean War. At least two-thirds of the deaths in this war had been due to disease – pneumonia, typhoid, cholera and gangrene – rather than wounds, and the sufferings endured by the soldiers aroused great concern. Florence Nightingale's success in caring for these stricken men convinced her that cleanliness, fresh (but not cold) air and sunlight, as well as regular attention and wholesome food, were vital for the care of the sick. Armed with international prestige as a result of her heroic efforts in the Crimea, she was then able to bring her experience and knowledge into the service of Britain at large.

Her *Notes on Hospitals* (1859) revolutionized hospital construction and management, and with the opening of the Nightingale Training School for Nurses at St Thomas's Hospital in London in 1860, she became the founder of modern nursing. As a result, hospitals became more civilized places and gradually even the wealthy, who had previously been treated as far as was possible at home, came to regard a stay in hospital as the best way of undergoing serious medical treatment. Another important result of the horrific Crimean War was the signing of the Red Cross Convention in Geneva in 1864.

The parallel efforts of the English surgeon, Joseph Lister, also contributed to greater safety and fewer fatalities within hospitals. In 1865 he discovered that if wounds were covered in dressings that had been soaked in phenol (carbolic acid), fewer of them subsequently became infected. (The stench from the open sores of infected patients had been one of the most unsavoury aspects of hospital atmospheres.) He

also recommended surgeons to wash their hands and surgical instruments in carbolic before starting to operate. Lister called carbolic acid an 'antiseptic' because it worked against sepsis, the infection of tissues by bacteria. He published many articles about his methods and the spray he invented to form a mist of antiseptic in the operating room and around the wound site became famous. Even so, many surgeons opposed his methods and resistance to antisepsis was complicated by the controversy which surrounded Pasteur's germ theory of disease, upon which Lister's methods were based.

The germ theory of disease

According to Pasteur's theory, living organisms originated only from other living organisms, and disease-causing organisms could be transmitted in the air. Opposing Pasteur was the theory of spontaneous generation, which suggested that the putrefaction of a wound was caused by organisms that were formed by the wound itself. In the 1860s Pasteur had set out to disprove this by an elegant series of experiments. In the best known of these, he poured some fermentable solution into a balloon-shaped flask fitted with a swan-neck. He then heated the solution for long periods in order to destroy any living organisms present in it. The flasks were then sealed and left for some time. After some months, the solution remained quite clear and no fermentation had taken place. After breaking the neck of some of the flasks, the liquid inside quickly became clouded. This experiment confirmed Pasteur's belief that what caused the infection of wounds was the living matter in the air of the laboratory.

Pasteur's theory and Lister's methods soon became accepted. (Lister received particularly strong support in Germany, where army surgeons tried his method with good results in the Franco-Prussian War of 1870.) As a result, mortality from

Florence Nightingale revolutionized the care of Crimean War casualties at the Military Hospital in Scutari (above). Before her regime soldiers were more likely to die of infection than wounds.

But this scene (right) from the Battle of Inkerman (1854) romanticizes a situation where drastic surgery was carried out without anaesthetics or antiseptics on the battle-field.

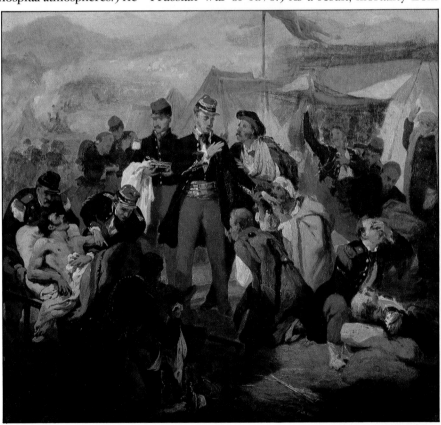

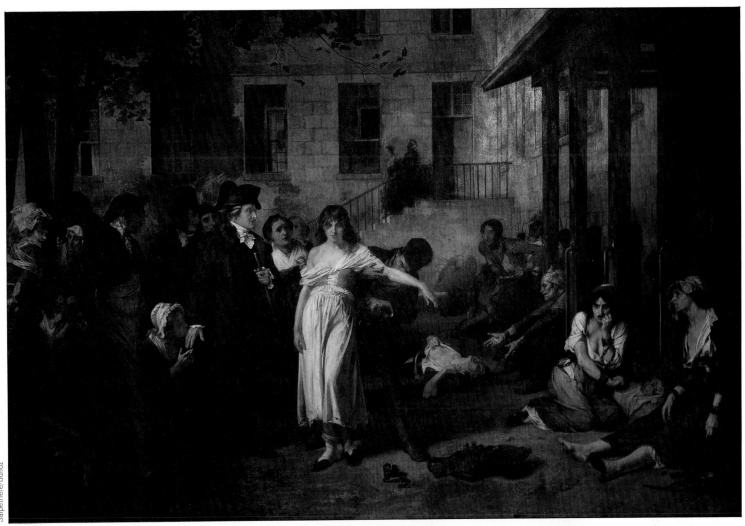

surgical sepsis fell dramatically, especially when it was realized that successful surgery required the exclusion of most bacteria from the operating room. Gradually, antiseptic surgery gave way to aseptic surgery, which involved the sterilization of everything that came into contact with the patient, together with strict cleanliness in all parts of the operating room. Lister's system tried to kill off bacteria before they could get into the patient's wound: aseptic methods ensured there were no bacteria there that needed to be killed. All these improvements effectively opened the door for more adventurous and more successful surgery.

Progress in vaccines

Pasteur's work on the germ theory also led him to develop the first effective vaccine since Edward Jenner's smallpox work in the late 18th century. Jenner had discovered that a person inoculated with the contents of a sore from the body of someone suffering from cowpox would not subsequently contract the deadly disease of smallpox. Pasteur's vaccine against rabies was more ingenious. He extracted the spinal cord of rabies-infected animals and hung them up to dry in his laboratory. By injecting the dried cord into animals, he discovered that if the cord was left for a long period of time, it lost most of its power to produce rabies in its next victim. Pasteur had discovered the principle of attenuation whereby an organism loses its infectivity and, what is more, the very same organisms then

Dr Pinel unshackles the wretched inmates of Paris's Salpêtrière Asylum in the late 18th century (above). This humane gesture marked a new approach to the treatment of 'lunatics'. Fifty years later, at the same asylum, Dr Charcot – hypnotizing a 'hysteric' (left) – further advanced medical strategies for the treatment of mental illness.

confer protection on the injected host.

Further new vaccines followed. In the 1880s the German microbiologist, Robert Koch, developed a vaccine against tuberculosis and his assistant, Emil Behring, produced one against diphtheria. At about this time, also, two American pharmacists, Henry Wellcome and Silas Burroughs, developed the first tabletted medicine. Until then, all medicines were made from the raw materials by the chemist or hospital apothecary and dispensed as powders, ointments or liquids. The problem was that it was not possible to know precisely how much of the drug was contained in each draught that was taken. The Burroughs Wellcome 'tabloid'-making machine solved the problem. It brought together exact quantities of ingredients into a compressed form. The tablet of medicine was thus born, and earned its inventors a great financial fortune.

By the end of the 19th century, medicine had become rooted in a firm scientific basis. It was still unable to offer much help against the more serious infectious diseases, but with more attention being paid to public health in Europe's major cities outbreaks were becoming less frequent and the diseases less often fatal. In the consulting room the doctor could draw upon a new and impressive range of gadgets to help him make a diagnosis. The laryngoscope could be used to examine the voice box and throat; the sphygmometer could be used to measure blood pressure; and the ophthalmoscope enabled the doctor to examine the back of the patient's eye. All these instruments were invented during the last few decades of the 19th century and, as if to herald the further advances of the 20th century, X-rays were discovered by William Röntgen in 1895 – an achievement for which the German scientist won the first Nobel Prize for physics in 1901.

Progress with mental health

One area of human health in which progress lagged behind until well into the 19th century was mental illness. Despite the sincere and, to a limited extent, effective efforts made by such individuals as Dr Pinel of the Salpêtrière Asylum in Paris and the Tuke family of Yorkshire in caring humanely for 'lunatics', their treatment on the whole remained clouded by ignorant, superstitious and even brutal attitudes. When matters improved it was due to several developments, but one conspicuously responsible individual was Jean-Martin Charcot, who took charge of the Salpêtrière, which was the largest mental asylum in Europe, in 1862.

By an especially careful and individual examination of the 3,000 distressed persons in his care, Charcot began to sort the mad from the epileptic, and patients who were seriously and permanently disturbed from people who were simply unable to cope with the problems of everyday life. In an age when mental illness was still associated with sin and evil, and when people suffering from all manner of mental disorders were often 'put away', this was an enlightened start. As a result of his approach Charcot and his colleagues isolated, among other conditions, a disease which they called 'multiple sclerosis' and a new awareness developed of the differences between physically- and psychically-derived disorders (even if psychological problems produced physical symptoms such as violent fits or paralysis).

Charcot became particularly renowned for his work on hysteria. As a state of over-anxiety characterized by excessive laughter or excessive crying, hysteria had long been thought of as an exclusively female disorder. But Charcot broadened the term to include many of the men in his care and, dismissing unscientific and lurid myths, he made progress through close observation and individual treatment of his 'hysteric' patients. For this work he often sent his patients into hypnotic trances by concentrating their attention on a fixed object, by putting gentle pressure on their eye-balls, by exposing them to the sounds of loud blows on a gong, or to bright lights. By this means he tried to treat the patient's psyche, having reached the 'unconscious' through hypnosis. And although Charcot's cures were seldom permanent, and his interpretations of the patients' behaviour under

Hotel de Ville/Lauros-Giraudon

hypnosis were often faulty, his influence was revolutionary. Sigmund Freud (1856–1939) was deeply impressed by Charcot's techniques and he began to use hypnosis as a means of bringing his clients' repressed memories to the surface.

During the 19th century concepts of illness, methods of treatment and knowledge of public health altered out of all recognition. Given the succession of 'miracles' that marked the century it is true to say that a person born in 1900 had a far greater chance of a healthy and comfortable life than a person born in 1800. However, it is also true that in the general enthusiasm for 'scientific' medicine many traditional healing practices were cast overboard as 'old wives' tales': today we are seeing a revival of many old medical practices in the form of 'alternative medicine'. Also, when the balance-sheet of medical progress is considered, it must be remembered that the great strides forward made in the 19th century only worked for the benefit of everyone when modern health services came into being.

A visit to a French hospital (above). This touching scene could not have taken place in the squalid hospitals of the early 19th century. Such an impeccable children's ward, with its clean linen and glistening floors, was the result of the tremendous advances made by medicine in the age of 'miracles'.

Index